The Gallant Mouth

The Gallant Mouth

Creating the educated equine mouth for all disciplines

Linda Kaye Hollingsworth-Jones

Katherine Grace Sutliff

Willow Grove Conservatory Press

ACKNOWLEDGMENTS

This book is the result of trying to become the teacher that horses and riders deserve. I wanted to create a work that could serve as a reference and an introduction to the ideas of Légèreté. Of course, I could not do this alone.

My dear husband, I can hardly take a breath without you. Thank you for walking through life with me and supporting me in every way. My boys, you are my heart. I know how lucky I am.

Huge thanks to Katie Sutliff for serving as my editor. Patient and detailed, she was the perfect choice to help me in so many ways!

My dear friends: You support the good in me. I can hardly believe my good fortune that you are in my life.

Many thanks to every horse whom I have been privileged to put my hands on and the owners who trusted me with them. Thank you to the people who have found my teaching helpful to them and supported me even when I was young and stupid.

Thanks to all my assistants and interns. Teaching you has taught me. I hope I brought something positive to your horsemanship journeys.

Thank you to my past instructors who challenged me with techniques and ideas and my current instructor who continues this path with me.

To my colleagues in the US and abroad who are also inspired by Légèreté, it is a joy to know you and network with you.

Many thanks to everyone behind the camera! The pros, Kelvin Watkins and Ashton Kingsley brought such great beauty to this work.

Mom and Dad. What else could you do with a horse-crazy girl? Exactly what you did. Thank you and love you forever.

INTRODUCTION

> "*But one cannot hope to teach this tact and delicate discernment which come only from practice... The classic authors, had they devoted volumes to the subject, could not thereby have produced a single horseman."*
> ~Dupaty de Clam (1744-1782)

Raised in southwest Idaho, part of the Great Basin horse culture, working horses and "gitttin' 'er dun," are part of my heritage as is the natural horsemanship movement which started with cowboys from this area. Over many years, I have ridden with trainers, both English and western, competing and winning at many disciplines. Yet something still seemed amiss. Where was the artistry? The intimacy of the dance? I couldn't see it in others and I couldn't feel it within my own riding. My heart, insatiable curiosity, and an overdeveloped sense of romanticism and fantasy had me looking out the window of the classroom, as it were, for that elusive pathway to something entirely different.

What I was hungry for was riding as an art form on the same level as that of playing a musical instrument. To elicit a pleasant sound when playing a musical instrument requires the study and mastery of hand movements, both big and small. The same can be said of other arts like painting, sculpting, and drawing. And so it is for the hand that applies rein aids felt by another being instead of an inanimate object. This instrument however is a thinking, feeling, sensing, moving being. The connection between the rider's hand and the horse's mouth, like the performance of music, can express layers, details.

It was when I began by riding with an instructor from France over the span of 6 years with multiple horses that I began to learn about Légèretè (French: lightness) and dug deep into the cultural, historical, technical, artistic, and applicable information contained within. In that time I began and continue to return to more and more source material that has been translated. In this way, it took a plethora of dead Frenchmen, and a couple of live ones, to illuminate the path that I'd been searching for, one which gave me a new appreciation for the complex possibilities of the human hand working artfully with the horse's mouth.

Staccato, diminuendo, fortissimo, pianissimo, accelerando, crescendo, leggiero, sforzando, tremolo, legato in music are to contact, communication, a dance in riding. Complete agreement. Coordination. Moves and counter moves. A series of unfortunate events. A puzzle. A detriment. Reassurance. An embrace. A projection of care and love.

I continue to develop my understanding and the "gossamer thread" of my hand to the mouth of the horse. Education, practice, mindfulness, patience, firmness, fluidity.

In this work, I focus on the human hand and the connection to the horse's mouth. This is enough to bring about a profound impact on the horse AND the rider. The artistry of the ecuyers (recognized, highly educated horsemen) who rest from their work in the depths of the earth will be resurrected one horse and one rider at a time. I write for the admiration of their work and the nobility of the horse.

" *"A strange art – music – the most poetic and precise of* "
all the arts, vague as a dream and precise as algebra." ~Guy
de Maupassant (1850-1893)

"À main galante, bouche galante."
A gallant hand to a gallant mouth

NOTE TO READERS

My biggest desire with this work is to inform you, the reader, that you and your choices matter. You and the horses you touch matter. You and your horses' health, inside and out, matters. You matter to your horse and vice versa. And you both matter to me.

I want to arm you with information; time-honed wisdom from centuries of ecuyers coupled with current scientific advancement. I'm not here to reinvent anything. I'm here to protect you from
short-sighted methods that harm your horse. My offering is the consolidation of all the books you don't have time to read and all the hours you don't have to ride different horses all day every day. I am distilling this into what I hope is a meaningful, educational and utilitarian way forward.

My goal with this book is not to portray perfection. The photos and the words will not be perfect. Perfection in equestrian studies is not a healthy goal to pursue. Perfection is destructive, driving us to unnatural and even cruel means with ourselves and our horses.

My goal is education and inspiration.
I believe you want the best for your horse.
I want the best for you both.

CONTENTS

CONTENTS

The Masters

> " *"There is an historical literature on the horse, that of equestrian professionals and that of historians, but they ignore each other. The first study history without knowing the tools, methodology and issues of social and cultural history, while the latter are not very interested in equestrian culture because they do not consider it part of the problem of the modern age, due to their ignorance of the current status of the horse and of their forgetfulness of its past importance." ~French historian Daniel Roche.* "

Church music from East Anglia (circa 1310-circa 1320) Llyfrgell Genedlaethol Cymru (National Library of Wales)

How can we understand music if we only look back 100 years instead of 1000? How can we understand how it grew and changed over time or how it was influenced by history and culture? We cannot adequately perform well what is ill-informed. We disrespect the works that have been handed to us by musicians throughout the centuries. For me, it is the same with equitation and all interaction with horses.

I see a clear parallel in the study and passion I have discovered among the ecuyers (learned horsemen) of history. Like court musicians and composers, life in the court (or the military) gave the ecuyer a stage on which to practice their craft. It also offered stability in their lives and the lives of their family. Excelling in these endeavors meant the difference between steady employment and distinction or poverty and anonymity. These are powerful motivators along with the devotion for their art.

In Medieval Europe, horse knowledge was passed on verbally from teacher to student. Think about the squire who worked fervently for a knight in hopes of becoming a knight himself. With the advent of the treatise in the Renaissance as well as the advances in book printing, techniques for riding, training, and horse care were available to an exponentially wider audience. Treatises began the process of a more expansive dialogue among ecuyers who may not have  had the chance to visit the riding hall of a renowned teacher. The insights of his work will live on being followed, maligned, built upon, clarified, or all of the above. As an American, I have difficulty comprehending the breadth and depth of the equine culture in Europe. It can be helpful to look at parallel times in history between Europe and North America.

There were great equine-centered festivals in Naples, Italy with highly trained horses around the time Christopher Columbus landed in the San Salvador Islands. The renowned Pignatelli was teaching in Rome when the first horses arrived in Florida with the Spanish. The equestrian treatise was becoming an accessible means of education, comparison, and interaction in Italy when the first colonies were being founded in North America. Two years before Plymouth Colony was founded, the first treatise in French was written and the great Ecole de Versaille (the court school of the king of France containing over 1000 royal horses) was founded. Gueriniere wrote the Bible of academic riding, "Ecole de Cavalerie" shortly after George Washington was born. Dupaty de Clam wrote his treatise the same year of the Revolutionary

War. In fact, the cavalry manuals for the US cavalry were taken from French military manuals.

Clearly, the populace of North America had more on their minds than the pursuit of the height of riding techniques. The methodologies used in North America were largely practical in nature: transportation, care and movement of livestock, and farming. The use of horses and their techniques were passed along mainly by direct observation or instruction as they were in the medieval era in Europe. A horseman could learn either by trial and error or by working side by side with the horseman they wanted to emulate. As we know by the game "telephone," alterations are inevitable in the passing of information. There was no concrete way to check exactly what the teacher may or may not have said or demonstrated.

When circumstances allowed for the luxury of education in riding, the techniques were imported from Europe along with the horses that they used- largely either of Spanish or English origin. The story for horsemen and women here in the US doesn't have to end there.

      "He who cannot draw on the past, is living from hand to mouth." ~Goethe

Second century manuscript of Xenophon's "Hellenica." Papyrus Museam of Venice. Works were transcribed by hand often on the backs of other works to save papyrus

The first written treatise concerning horses and their training was by Simon of Athens (5th c. BC) and the well-known Xenophon (3rd c. BC). Xenophon's work is the only one that has survived largely intact. The Dark Period follows in equestrian literature but as the Renaissance (generally considered the 14th-17th centuries) swept through Europe with ideologies of science and art, we find the development of a new form of literature: the treatise on horses, riding, farriery, veterinary medicine, combat, and general care.

The first treatise after the Dark Period was by King Dom Duarte I of Portugal (ca. 1391-1438). "The Instruction of the Art of Riding in Every Saddle" was first printed in 1434. From this point, this new form of literature arises mainly in Italy. Far from appearing from thin air, it was merely the writing down of the established practices of equitation (riding and all it entails) already complex and refined. Looking back, this is already 600+ years of collective wisdom!

> " *"I consider above all Sir Federico Grisone, who first wrote,* "
> *and certainly divinely...about the rules of riding, because up*
> *to the present time, not one dared before him to face this*
> *undertaking..." ~Claudio Corte (born 1514)*

In Padoua, appresso Gratioso Perchacino.
Title page of Grisone's "Rules of Riding," 1550

Frederico Grisone wrote the first treatise that became the book on every nobleman's shelf, "The Rules of Riding" published in 1550. With this, the genre of equitation treatises began. His work was followed by Fiaschi, Pignatelli, and other Italians. The French, and others, took the knowledge they learned in Italy and returned with it to the courts of their respective countries. Inevitably cultural and current events altered the work bringing about unique regional ideologies. My interests and education took me to the French ecuyers and the passing of knowledge and experience down the generations through the French courts and military riding schools.

The new genre of literature made its way to France with the first works written in French by Salomon de la Broue and Antoine Pluvinel, both students of the Italian, Pignatelli. Together they would become the foundation of the old French haute école (high school). Their methods shifted from the sometimes rough practices of the Italians to kinder and more thoughtful methods, drawing the horse into participation and treating the horse with the utmost respect.

Engraving by Crispin de Pas from "The Maneige Royal" by Antoine de Pluvinel

Salomon de la Broue focused on quietness in hand, mobility, and lightness. Pluvinel, more widely known, focused on the psychology of the horse, their individuality, and the realization that the horse should take pleasure in his work. From these two men (and others) came generations of ecuyers who both embraced and refined the works of the men that came before them.

These men and others taught in the courts of nobles as well as teaching the military. This was common throughout Europe. My research points to riding schools in France emphasizing the artistry of riding even for combat uses more so and for longer than the other countries and cultures beginning at the court of Versaille and continuing through the work of the cavalry school at Saumur. In addition, the French championed and cherished Légèreté, or lightness, in their work with horses. A horse that is light is eager to respond to a request without fear or tension. It is a delicate balance but one, I believe, was central to French equitation in all its facets.

The reason I have continued to so deeply explore this tradition has much to do with the Tableau assembled by René Bacharach (at the end of this chapter). As I read each name I saw their connection or employ, whom they were influenced by, whom they influenced, and what works they wrote. I realized a serendipitous and unique combination of a place in history, geography, support from court or state, leadership, devotion, exactitude, loyalty, interconnectedness, and esteem. From this arose a honed set of techniques directly from the manège (academic, often indoor riding arena), tried in the fires of sometimes hostile disputes, discourses, and open insubordination. These circumstances added up to the advancement of the art of equitation (the education of horse and rider) and a celebration of the horse and all he entails. A culture of schooling a horse for charging into battle or presenting Haute Ecole (The High School; very advanced maneuvers) before a king. I don't believe this occurred to this degree anywhere else in history.

I applaud UNESCO for declaring French equitation as an Intangible Cultural Heritage because of the distinct impact of this cumulative body of work. Silke Rottermann reporting on the Inscription by UNESCO said it well, "The importance of French traditional equitation as a part of a centuries-old equestrian culture is without a doubt shown in the UNESCO inscription since 2011. However, the inscription alone is not sufficient to secure the continuity of a riding style. Paper doesn't blush. A style dies out or lives on not because its protection on paper, but through its representatives." That's why I'm studying, riding, reading, teaching, and writing about it.

Many, if not most notable ecuyers strove to codify their discoveries in writing and pass on the wisdom they had gained over their lifetimes of daily immersion in horses and highest academic equitation. You can study the ideas of any ecuyer by reading their work, the work of their master, and possibly the master before that! You can read the work of multiple students of a great master to see what idiosyncrasies may have come about in the passing of the baton to his students. The words, the experience, the techniques are all in print. Finding them translated into English may be your only barrier.

Some of the treatises contained the work of a devoted student who would write to clarify the teachings of his master. An example is Faverot de Kerbrech in his book "Methodical Dressage of the Riding Horse" subtitled "From the last teaching of François Baucher as recalled by one of his students." Other treatises contained thinly veiled insults and challenges passed back and forth among contemporaries.

The story that displayed most clearly to me the passion, dignity, and pride ecuyers took in their work is the challenge James Fillis (1834-1913) leveled against Captain Jacques Saint- Phalle (1867-1908) in the year 1904. Fillis, an Englishman educated in France, accused Saint-Phalle of placing himself and his abilities above the great masters without

James Fillis shows canter on three legs

giving them proper respect. Both Fillis and Saint- Phalle had written their own treatises, the latter having done so when he was only 32 years old. Fillis published his book when he was in his 50s.

The Courbette is one of the three traditional airs of the Cadre Noir. Saint-Phalle takes it one step further with Courbette in tandem.

Things became heated between them and included public criticism, public explanations, and even printed pamphlets stirring up the European horse world. Finally, the gauntlet was thrown down by Fillis: Saint-Phalle was to execute the fantasy airs he boasted of mastering in public with a jury of 3 ecuyers and a photographer. Saint-Phalle, suffering from overwork from preparing his horses, Theo and Iran, presented the three-legged canter, canter backward, and flying change of lead backward. A document signed by Captain Lafont was sent to Fillis along with the photographs. Saint-Phalle's exhaustion worsened and he died in a sanatorium with only enough time to finish his second book. I think it is worthy of note that Captain de Saint-Phalle had earlier won the first Cavalry Horse Championship (which would become eventing) in 1902.

This story could be seen as tragic or triumphant. Or perhaps both. What drives someone to be so deeply invested in their craft? Saint-Phalle was known as an extremely hard worker consumed by reading hundreds of books. He would stay up late writing notes on his horses and their progress. He spent many hours in the saddle beyond the required rehearsals and

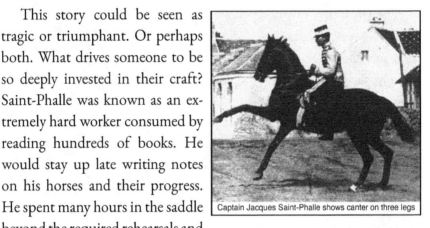

Captain Jacques Saint-Phalle shows canter on three legs

teaching he was assigned as a Captain in the Cadre Noir. He loved to experiment beyond even the movements of the Haute Ecole. He taught his own horses the fantasy airs of trotting and cantering backward and cantering on 3 legs. Are these airs useful? Not particularly. But he loved what he did. He was consumed by it, literally. These are the kinds of men I want to draw inspiration and education from.

> "When [the mouth] is formed and reduced to a just temper [put in tune] and the hand knows how to play upon it, they will find that not only a snaffle but even a ribbon or packthread will be sufficient to guide and control the animal in all its motions." ~de la Gueriniere

From the first works in Italy to the later works in France, treatises on horse education unfailingly addressed the hand of the rider and the mouth of the horse. Entire books can be seen from the period devoted to bits and bitting. These bits may seem harsh or extreme to us today but for the purposes the horses were serving and the training methods used, these worked well (enough). By the time of de La Gueriniere, bits were becoming simpler, and instructions concerning the use of the hand clear.

What was universal throughout these works was the clarity of the aids (hands, legs, voice, whip, etc) because of the respect due to the horse. The education of the rider included a firm and supple seat to support not only his balance but also to stabilize his body to enable sophisticated and nuanced use of his hands.

For a horse to be light, the horse must clearly understand what is being asked of him. Without understanding, we draw tension, resistance, fear, or frustration from the horse. This is why I am so passionate about the rider's hand, the horse's mouth, and the education of the bit. The human hand is our most sophisticated and delicate instrument. The same is true of the horse's mouth. When they come together it can be artistry or agony. The difference is an education system that builds clarity.

William Cavendish Duke of Newcastle (1592-1676) François Baucher 1796-1873 James Fillis (1834-1913) Henry de Bussigny (1840-1922) Jean Froissard (1923-?)

Horses were educated from the ground from the beginning. You simply cannot walk up to an unlearned horse, hop on and ride away. Teaching the horse the necessary prerequisites was a matter of common sense. There can be more than just "getting by" so we can ride. There are concepts, actions, sensations, cooperation, clarity, and relaxation that can be gained by teaching the horse from the ground.

Cavendish described and depicted the process of teaching even complicated airs to the horses from the ground before doing so under saddle. Baucher was well known for expanding on bit work in hand to decrease resistance and increase relaxation and release of the mouth and jaw. It would be fair to say that Baucher was a catalyst for more in-depth work from the ground with the bit. His influence can still be felt through those that followed. Fillis, Bussigny, DeCarpentry, Froissard, Karl, and other Frenchmen followed suit while including variations based on their own experience. It continues with ecuyers today.

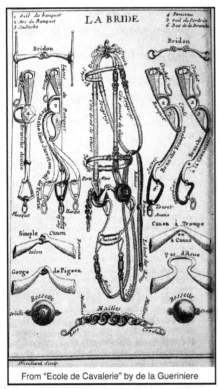

From "Ecole de Cavalerie" by de la Gueriniere

You can ride bitless, bridle-less, whatever you like. It doesn't bother me at all. I do those things for variety from time to time. But throughout the ages volumes have been written about the hand and the mouth. Bitting. Contact. Feel. Softness. It can vary with the dis-cipline, culture, and use of the horse. My background in music has sent me to the time and culture where I see the most interchange of ideology about the hand and the mouth as well as the lifting up of the education of the horse and rider in the most overall horse friendly manner: the French tradi-tion often referred to as Légèreté.

The renaissance of France con-tains an interchange of riders that continued forward through their students and their students for 3 or more centuries. Often these ecuyers agreed. Sometimes they vehemently disagreed. But they interacted with one another creating a proving ground within the court (Versailles) the military (Saumur) or even the circus. The writings that they left behind can give us a picture of their education process, their priorities, their successes. These writings need to be read in context. Who was the author? What position did they hold in society? Where were they living? Why did they write the book? What kind of horses were they riding? What was the purpose of the education of the horse? Who was their intended audience? Without context, grievous mistakes can be made in the interpretation of the work.

So we take the work of these long-dead masters and somehow their love, passion, and wisdom receive a second breath. They receive the respect and audience they deserve, we receive the advantage of literally lifetimes of work with horses. Add the filter of today's science for refinement of techniques that we may now understand to be less than ideal, and you literally have the very best of past and present to offer our horses and the future.

" *"Equitation that is beautiful, delicate, and tasteful, seeks* "
the development of this beauty by relying on the very gifts o
the horse and not by rendering them unnatural. It is nature
that this equitation takes as a guide and not the extraordi-
nary or the eccentric that is sought." ~Alexis-François
L'Hotte (1825-1904)

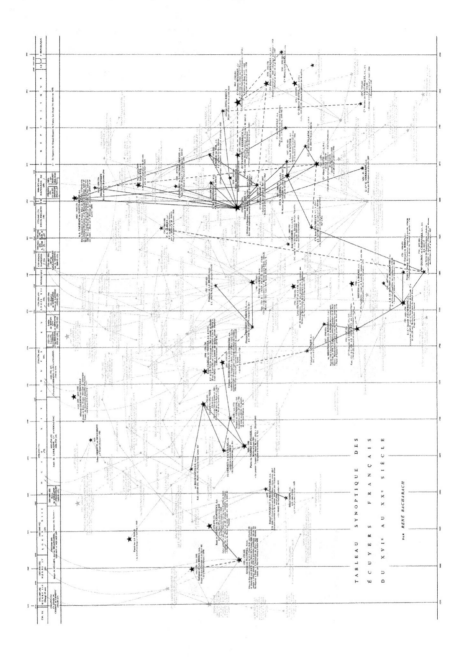

TABLEAU SYNOPTIQUE DES
ÉCUYERS FRANÇAIS
DU XVIᵉ AU XXᵉ SIÈCLE
PAR RENÉ BACHARACH

2

The Human Hand

" "Behold the hands, how they promise, conjure, appeal, menace, pray, supplicate, refuse, beckon, interrogate, admire, confess, cringe, instruct, command, mock and what not besides, with a variation and multiplication of variation which makes the tongue envious." ~Montaigne "

It is obvious that our hands can do unimaginable deeds of great good or great evil. History tells us as much. For our uses, we will leave the realm of philosophy and focus our study on the human hand. What is it? How does it work? How can we use it to create rich communication with our horse?

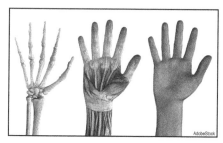

The hand is the world's most complex, sophisticated tool, so ideal in its design that we cannot yet duplicate its innumerable functions. The hand contains 29 bones, 34 muscles (much of the articulation of the hand is controlled by muscles in the forearm), 100 ligaments and tendons, 3 major nerves, and two major arteries. The entire hand has about 100,000 lesser nerves of at least 20 different kinds. More than 3000 touch receptors inhabit each fingertip to relay information concerning heat, cold, texture, pressure, movement, and pain to an extremely high degree. The nerve fiber density in the fingertips is the highest in the entire body. It is over twice that of the rest of the fingers and nearly 5 times that of the palm of the hand. It is incomparable.

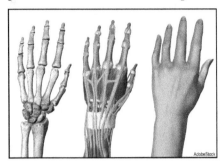

With all of this in mind, why would we overlook the possibilities we, well, hold in our hands? If we focus on all of the functions available, we can truly speak and listen with our hands! Remember, the horse's nerve densities are as developed as ours! They can also feel the tiniest input as we can. I remember clearly being told, "If a horse can be bothered by a fly, he can feel the lightest of aids." That speaks to the sensitivity of the equine skin. When we address him through a bit we are speaking to the ultimate sensitivity of the horse's mouth.

"The hand is the tool of tools." Aristotle

The Classical Period in Ancient Greece produced some of the greatest minds of all time. Philosopher and polymath, Aristotle, could see the hand as unrivaled in complexity and utility. This evaluation changed little through the ages.

During the Renaissance (approximately 1300 AD-1600 AD) The human hand was viewed not only in literal terms but also as a symbol of the enlightenment; the most powerful avenue to bring thoughts to form. It's no coin-

cidence that the hand played a central role in equitation as it blossomed in Italy and France during the same time period! It only made sense to work diligently with the "tool of tools" until it approached the "gallant hand" spoken of by the great horsemen of the time.

The hand continues into the 21 century to be a subject of study among artists and scientists. Research continues to discover the nearly unbelievable abilities of our hands and fingertips.

"The study (from the KTH Royal Institute of Technology in Stockholm, Sweden) marks the first time that scientists have quantified how people feel, in terms of a physical property. One of the authors, Mark Rutland, Professor of Surface Chemistry, says that the human finger can discriminate between surfaces patterned with ridges as small as 13 nanometres in amplitude and non-patterned surfaces."

Thirteen nanometers! To gain a perspective on that length, a sheet of paper is 100,000 nanometers thick! There is a reason that mankind has been in awe of the human hand for centuries.

"The human hand allows the mind to reveal itself." - Maria Montessori

Stop and think on this for just a few moments. As broad as the mind can think, believe, imagine, plan, devise, create, it is the hand that is responsible to bring it to the physical world. The possibilities are nearly endless. Achieving basic competence at any skill takes time and effort!

Each person in the photographs (next page) is someone in my life doing amazing things with their minds and hands. We can easily understand the years it takes to learn and apply any of these skills on a basic level. Just how long does it take to achieve mastery? Years? Decades? Why should the expectation be any less for the education of our minds and hands when interacting directly with a horse's mouth?

Hands at work and play: From top, left to right: My nephew Patrick juggling, sister CJ Wilky-bladesmith, Charlie working on a knife, Dad with his camera, Dad restoring an antique, Adrienne Hendricks-saddle maker, Charlie-cardshark, CJ-Knitting, Me-drawing, Me-archery, Paul Tillotson-Jazz pianist, Tim Waddle-Chef, Louise Owen-Violinist, Joanna Robertson-Message Therapist, David Eames-Farrier, Dr. James Thomson caring for my newborn nephew.

The horse's mouth is not an inanimate object like a violin. The violin waits to be played and reflects exactly the technique from the hand. You can practice on a violin for hours and the violin doesn't mind even if you make mistakes and play wrong notes. With enough skill in the hands that play it, a simple violin can create beautiful music. But if the plain violin isn't seen for the music it can create, its value is not seen. What if someone had the privilege to play a Stradivarius? Would it be treated like the priceless instrument it is? It takes even greater skill to rise to the level this instrument deserves. This is how I perceive our work with the horse's mouth.

I will continue with more details in the chapter on the horse's mouth, but all those statistics on the human hand and how sensitive it is? The horse's lips and tongue are their versions of their hands. If an action would make your hand uncomfortable, it's making your horse's mouth uncomfortable. We'll discuss that a little later.

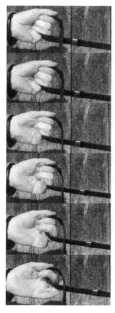

I'm hoping that it is clearly evident that the education of the hand (including fingers, wrist, elbows, and shoulders) in following the mouth is a substantial undertaking. So why do it? Why not ride with a loose rein? You can if you choose. But you are missing out on the subtleties of communication available through the hand and mouth. It's not easy, but what worthwhile thing is? The next obvious question is how to do it.

Let's begin with basic rein handling. Clearly, the rein is in direct communication with the bit and the horse's very sensitive mouth and lips. The hand is the most articulate of any portion of our body including our arms. It truly is our "tool of tools" for both speaking and listening to our horse. Think about it like this: how many delicate, minute things would we be able to do without our hands? Not many. If we think about the education of the hands in isolation, we can compare it to bowing technique and fingering for the violin or scales on the piano. Having our hands and fingers supple and working correctly takes time and effort *even before we include the horse and his movements!*

A good starting position with the rein is stabilizing the rein between the thumb and pointer finger. This prevents the length of rein from changing accidentally by slipping. The other fingers form a spring system. They open and close as needed at various speeds, intensities, and strengths to communicate the request to the horse or follow the horse's mouth. (It is your preference if you wish to enclose the reins with three fingers or four.) The basic position is closed fingers in order to potentially give the most amount possible with the fingers. If the fingers are already partially open, there is less distance the fingers can go before they are straight. If the fingers are completely open, the spring system is already sprung. if the fingers are stiff and unyielding, then there simply is no spring system, no shock absorbing between the hand and the horse's mouth.

While focusing on the hand, we can clearly see that the reins can be shortened and lengthened several inches simply by the opening and closing of the fingers. This skill set is best utilized as a practiced, automatic response in the hand, able to keep a light tension on the reins in all degrees of open and closed while never reaching a place of the fingers being fully straight. Not only does the completely straight finger nullify any shock-absorbing or spring effect between the arm and the horse's mouth, but it also forces the rider to depend on the much larger and less articulate movements of the arm to communicate. It would be like painting with your elbow. You simply need the intricacy of the fingers and the wrist to interact in a subtle, clear way. As I said above, these opening/closing movements starting from the pinky and moving toward the middle finger, can happen as slow or as quickly as needed. That takes time to develop, like practicing scales on the piano. At first, you play them slowly to learn them correctly. Then you increase the speed without losing the quality of the movements. Slow movements, as well as quick ones, will be necessary to play various musical pieces on the piano. Slow and quick movements are also necessary for communicating clearly with your horse!

The fingers are the center of subtlety in the rein aids but there are additional movements of the wrist and forearm that can support or extend the actions of the fingers. The use of the wrist can enhance the shock-absorbing functions of the contact by adding another spring to the overall system. It's not nearly the difference that the fingers can make, but a supple wrist can offer further agility in either following the mouth or stabilizing the contact with the horse.

Keep in mind, the further we get from the fingers, the ultimate communicators when well prepared, the less refined the aid will be. Therefore, the wrist, the elbow, and slight movements through the shoulders will be less and less dextrous. The muscles of the hand are designed for intricate movement. The muscles of the arm and shoulder are, as a friend paraphrases, big, stupid muscles. They are designed for large, less precise movements that are more clumsy and less clear. This is why I don't depend on them as my main aids through the reins. Again I return to the remarkable hand.

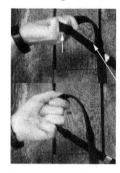

Unlike what you see commonly in the horse world today, the primary movement of the forearm is one of lifting to create an effect on the bit in the corners of the mouth, not on the tongue or the bars. In the equitation treatises of the 16th-19th centuries, this is made clear by the instruction to "lift the hands and turn the wrists so the fingernails are facing up." What these ecuyers understood was the negative impact pulling had on the entire workings of the horse. The addition of twisting your wrist to bring the fingernails up extends the movement a bit more without lifting the entire arm.

Now here is where folks start to develop a rash in the lifting of the hand so I'll go ahead and address it here. The lifting of the hand/forearm (instead of pulling backward) is 1. A more friendly aid in the horse's mouth by not acting on the tongue/bars. 2. An infinitely more controllable move-ment in the muscles lifting the

Does this arm position look familiar? It does because it is the best position to balance something with equilibrium and coordination. Think, "don't spill the wine!"

forearm than the ones we use to pull the arms backward. The muscles to pull the arms backward are designed for strength and force. This is NOT what we want to use on horses' mouths. 3. A far superior position of the arm and hand to carry something valuable. The arms,

Henri III taught by la Broue (c.1530-c.1610)

Pluvinel (1556-1620)

Bellegarde (mid 16th century)

Cavendish (1592-1676)

de la Gueriniere (1688-1751)

von Sind (1709-1776)

Dupaty de Clam (1744-1782)

Baucher (1796-1873)

Fillis (1834-1913)

Beudant (1863-1949)

Decarpentry (1878-1956)

Lesage (1885-1968)

The lifting of the hand (instead of pulling) is standard procedure for generations of ecuyers. It may look odd to the modern eye but it has been in use for centuries.

in this bent position, are best prepared to articulate balance and safety (think carrying a tray of drinks or a baby. You would involuntarily lift your arms a bit to ensure the best muscles are in play for the task with buoyancy and room to readily and quickly adjust as needed.)4.

The higher position gives us ample room to lower our arms when the horse reaches into the bit. It offers a more inviting, encouraging feeling for the horse to seek the contact. 5. Once our Request is answered by the horse, we relax and may lower the hand to a more commonly seen position. This, in the French tradition, is referred to as *descente de main* (literally translated: lower the hand. A more accurate translation in this use is to *stop acting with the hand*. Andre Jessaume uses the word "surrender" the hand which is also an interesting translation.) We act in an upward action but we won't be riding with our hands in the air forever.

Ecuyers knew this and utilized it openly in their work. If you consider the hundreds of years of the study of the education of horses, the low hand or a hand that pulls back is a new approach. It is also decidedly not considerate of the horse. I reach again into musical references for a parallel: playing techniques, including hand and arm position, have remained largely unchanged over the centuries simply because those techniques have been proven to be most effective, efficient, and allow for the most artistic expression. It doesn't mean you can't play the piano by opening the lid and strumming the strings, it's just not how the piano was designed. Rest assured your piano teacher will ensure you have good basic techniques before you begin to experiment. If not, you don't have a foundation on which to build. In both music and horsemanship, innovation for nothing more than the sake of innovation is novel at best and harmful at worst. Innovation for the sake of winning is decidedly questionable, especially when another being is involved.

> " *"Fine art is that in which the hand, the head, and the heart of man go together." ~John Ruskin* "

I do believe in art and science. These are the elements that make up the hand, head, and heart. I have come to realize that if any of these elements is missing, the result lacks balance, like a stool with only two legs. In my pursuit of what is worthy of our gifts (as well as those of the horse), the greatest offering is our dedication to utmost excellence in the coordination, subtlety, clarity, respect, and consistency of the requests we make through our hands. My hope is that we will educate and elevate the skill of our hands to earn the respect of our horse's mouth. Our hands are capable of initiating a conversation by asking as well as listening to the horse's reply.

3

The Horse's Mouth

I remember Buck vividly. He was my first equine teacher. A late teens gray Quarter Horse, Arabian cross gelding with quite the life story before I came along. I know I was lucky to have the Local Living Legend to ride and learn from!

His experiences included many horse shows of all kinds, Eh Capa Bareback Riders (a riding team that rides bareback and bridleless), trail riding, swimming in the river, goat tying, gymkhana events, and rodeo queening (his owner became Miss High School Rodeo America!). He was even used as a model in two of Robert Vavra's beautiful books: "All Those Girls in Love with Horses" and "All the Unicorns I Have Known." He was a celebrity. He was especially good at teaching young punks like me how to respect his experience and education. I was so in awe of him and my grand good fortune, I spent hours piled high and deep riding, brushing, cleaning stalls, watching him graze, sitting on him in the moonlight. I was familiar with his mismatched ears, (one having a notch in the tip), the scar on his right shoulder and V branded into his left hip. The gradient tones of his mane faded from gray to white as you looked from near his head to his withers. It was similar to his tail: gray at the top and white at the bottom. I kept a wary eye out for any little bump on his black skin (he regularly had melanomas removed). I even knew he had low socks on all four legs and a star on his forehead that you could only see when he was wet or spotlessly clean. Even with all the time I spent with him, the mouth was simply an unknown.

Adobe stock photo

Adobe stock photo

I could see his incisors when he grazed or when I just played with his lips. I could feel his tongue when I inserted my thumb into his mouth to encourage him to open up for the bit. I loved the feeling of his lips as he gathered and enjoyed tasty tidbits from my hand. Yet I still had precious little knowledge or understanding of the structure and workings of the equine mouth. Now I realize how devastatingly limiting it was to me and my horsemanship growth. I have come to see how understanding the complexities of the horse's mouth is essential to building communication between the rider and the horse through the bit.

"More than any other skeletal feature, the skull is a great source of information about an animal's environment lifestyle." ~Glenn Searfoss

It seems reasonable to become at least a little familiar with the skull. It surrounds the mouth and its connective structures. The equine skull has both resiliency and vulnerability. Even though it's not a complex mechanism with the single joint of the jaw, it can still become dysfunctional for a myriad of reasons. The skull is comprised of the Mandible (lower jaw)

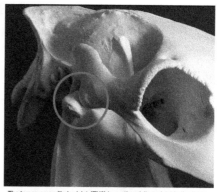

The temporomandibular joint (TMJ) is a rather delicate joint in the horse. It has just a cartilage disc separating the mandible from the maxilla and can suffer from osteoarthritis and other changes from excessive age or use.

and the Maxilla (upper jaw). The Maxilla is 34 bones very closely knit together. Although they are connected, they still have a small amount of mobility. Horses can have temporomandibular joint (TMJ) issues as well as cranial imbalances that can be negatively affected by impact trauma, muscle tension in the face or neck, or inappropriate use of the bit.

The mouth of the horse is exquisitely designed to purpose: the lips locate and decipher food choices. The incisors clip it off when grazing. The tongue moves the food to the molars to chew and then continues to push chewed food to the back of the mouth to swallow. The tongue also moves around the teeth and cheeks to clear out stray bits of food and keep the teeth clean. It is a very efficient and effective system.

The exterior of the mouth consists of the lips, both on the side and in front. The lips on the side create a funnel for food to be gathered into the mouth (and for the mouth to be able to open and close). The front lips are the explorers, like our fingers. The lips can sort a grain from surrounding sand, decipher what is good to eat and what isn't, learn how to unlatch gaits or untie their friends. The exterior mouth also functions in social ways, the Flehmen response, tensing with frustration, baring the teeth to intimidate, gapping with submission, wiggling to scratch a friend.

The interior mouth contains teeth and soft tissues. We are usually aware of the mouth we can see but in its entirety, it runs nearly the entire length of the skull. The soft tissues consist of the tongue, palate, gums, interior of the cheek, interior of the lips, and other areas of the oral mucosa. These structures are the most highly innervated sur-

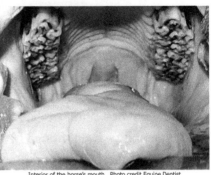

Interior of the horse's mouth. Photo credit Equine Dentist

faces of the entire horse, not unlike our fingertips. Like our fingertips, the structures of the mouth can feel motion, temperature changes, texture, pressure, taste (on the tongue), and pain. Because of the density of nerves in the tongue and mouth, strong sensory experiences can be excruciating. Think of hitting your finger with a hammer or getting it pinched in a car door. That's what the horse is experiencing with downward or backward acting pressure on the tongue.

The foremost third of the tongue is highly mobile which can cause dismay when the horse waggles it out the side of the mouth or continues to put it over the bit. These are evasions from the bit usually caused by previous painful experiences. Many horse people will try to shut the mouth with a cavesson and call the job done. The expression from the horse is still there under the "muzzle" of the cavesson. We would like to work in such a way that the horse need not utilize such extreme expressions.

The tongue, at its base, is connected to the Hyoid apparatus situated in between the horse's jawbones. The Hyoid is attached to the skull and supports a network of muscle attachments in the jaw and neck even serving to aid the opening of airways during exercise. For decades I put horses in various head and neck positions with little regard to the positive or negative chain of events that would ensue. I now see how short-sighted this is. It blinds the horseman as he blissfully believes he is training correctly while debilitating the horse's correct use of his body.

The truth of the matter is the tongue/hyoid/body connection affects the locomotion of the horse.

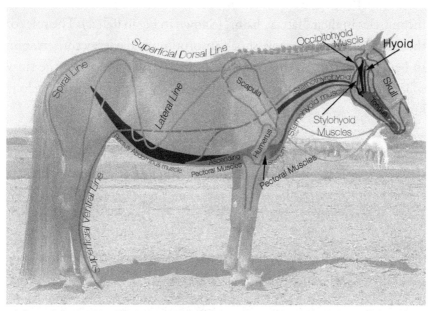

A few of the multitude of connections between the tongue/hyoid and the entire body of the horse. When there is a problem in the mouth, it travels, directly affecting the locomotion and biomechanics of movement.

The hyoid apparatus is the means, through muscle and fascia attachments, of transference of motor and sensory input from the tongue to the body. The hyoid influences the pelvis through a direct attachment to the sternum (sternohyoid muscle) which is, in turn, directly connected to the pelvis (Pectorals/rectus abdominus). The hyoid influences the extension of the shoulder and protraction of the front leg through the direct connection of the brachiocephallic muscle. Cadaver studies in horses have demonstrated the direct influence the hyoid and tongue have on the correct function of the hind leg through the fascia system. It is obvious the mouth of the horse is central to our clear understanding of communicating through the bit.

The fascia is not a commonly discussed area of anatomy or biomechanics. The fascia of an animal, including horses, encases and connects muscles and muscle groups together like a web. It acts as a means of synchronization of muscles as they work. So muscles are NOT functioning in isolation but in intimate coordination with all of the muscles in their "fascia chain." (Shown in Fig in italics). The roles of the fascia can include recoil, shock absorption, and energy conservation to be used later in an expression of power. There's more to the story of interconnectedness in horses than meets the eye of even the lifelong horseman!

"The head and neck are the door through which one takes possession of the house that is the horse. The mouth is the fragile lock of this door and the cession de mâchoire (relaxed movement of the jaw) is its key. You only need your legs if you want to kick the door open ... " ~Dominique Olivier

I feel compelled to point out here Olivier's reference to the fragile lock of the mouth. The interior of the mouth is the most innervated of the entire horse. The bars of the mouth (the part of the jaw above where the bit sits) are narrow and very sharp. If the tongue doesn't stay under the bit or the action of the bit is

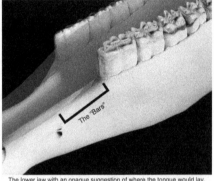

The lower jaw with an opaque suggestion of where the tongue would lay. You can see how narrow the bone of the interdental space is, aka the "bars."

too harsh, the bit surface comes into contact with the bars and can easily cause intense pain, even fractures. One study revealed *interdental bone spurs in 88% of bitted working horses!*

The entirety of the interior mouth structure is thickly laden with nociceptors and easily bruised, lacerated, and ulcerated. Another tactic horses use to decrease overall net pain is to put the tongue behind or over the bit. This simply need not happen with intelligent use of the hand! It's evident our first job is to not inflict pain with our communication!

The mouth is indeed a very fragile lock and with its interconnectedness throughout the horse, the relaxation of the tongue and jaw is the key.

"...the hand's first duty is to develop, improve and safeguard a soft mouth. The disappearance of this quality in the mouth instantly affects the horse's general behavior and his performance of movements and gaits."
~Jean Froissard

When the tongue is relaxed, it will lay flat and softly along the lower mandible resting against the palate and the back of the front lower incisors. This allows for normal breathing and swallowing. if the horse is comfortable and remains relaxed while carrying a bit, the tongue, basically a mass of muscles, will carry the bit allowing it to sink slightly into the tongue in the space between the tongue and the upper palate. If the tongue is drawn back toward the gullet/throat, it not only creates tension, it leaves the fragile bars vulnerable to direct interaction with the bit. The tongue can move the bit, play with the bit, lift and drop the bit, adjust it to be comfortable. The bars have no ability to change the position of the bit for comfort. Each horse has a unique mouth conformation but intelligent use of simple bits is the best way to ensure comfort and clarity with any horse. Just as the relaxation of the tongue travels through the body, so does any tension in the tongue.

With this in mind, the actions of our hands to the horse's mouth should convey a clear request without abruptness, brute force (by pulling backward or using highly leveraged bits), or abrasive sensations from harsh mouthpieces. There is no reason for a horse to trust himself through his most intimate and sensitive area if it is repeatedly a negative experience for him.

Education of such a complex system should be clearly undertaken by an intelligent hand and not restricting, dictatorial, inanimate gadgets such as side reins or draw reins. These do not offer intelligent release or relief from a fixed position. Both put pressure directly on the sensitive tongue and bars. Both encourage the horse to come to any means necessary to relieve the discomfort of the action by coming behind the bit, over-flexing, putting the tongue over the bit, out the side of the mouth, or drawing it up and behind the bit. Not only is the horse trying to save his own mouth, the fixed and often extreme positions he is asked to hold cause muscle fatigue, cramping, restricted airways, compression of the parotid glands, hyperextension of the nuchal ligament (that can cause tearing of insertion points) and massive amounts of tension and anxiety. Do we want our horses to learn how to join in the dance or do we simply want to dominate them, bullying them into pointless, even damaging positions?

"Action without reflection is but agitation." ~French saying.

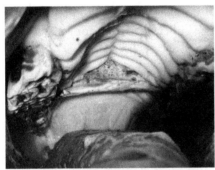

"Out of sight, out of mind," can easily occur with the mouth. A stick had become wedged across the palate of this horse between the base of the molars. It was removed and the horse's mouth treated and rebalanced. It is truly difficult to actually see the workings of the interior of the mouth but that doesn't negate our responsibility to act in accordance with its sensitivity.

The multitude of details we have covered presses us on to do the best we can to protect and educate our hands and the mouth of the horse. This reality has been at the forefront of the minds of ecuyers for centuries. Sometimes the equipment wasn't what we would choose to use today in light of the variety of bits we have available in our time. Regardless, the goal remains the same. A more positive approach is to begin the education of the human hand and the horse's mouth from the ground.

While standing on the ground you are working from a position the horse finds innately familiar (unless you frequently see other animals riding your horse without your permission). From the ground you are stable, can see what your hands are doing (a basic level of neurofeedback), can immediately see the horse's response, adjust your input as needed, and learn what that response feels like (awareness). Once you're on the horse's back, you only have this "feel" to go by so why not inform it and tune it in the way that is easiest for both you and your horse?

From the ground, we can explain that the odd object in his mouth is not there to antagonize or cause pain but to relax and inform. In essence, we can turn the action of the bit into a relaxation button by associating understood movements of the bit to the cession de machoire (relaxed movement of the mouth followed by swallowing.) We are teaching the horse the message, "I am here. I am listening. You can trust me. Let's do this together." Emotional and physical relaxation follow and the whole experience becomes positive for both the horse and rider. Because the horse is rarely volunteering for his education (much-preferring eating and sleeping), I believe the priority should be his benefit in every way.

The work from the ground is also a good process to rehabilitate and reeducate horses who show pathological issues from past trauma, tension, anxiety, insecurity, or a multitude of other concerning behavior with the mouth and the bit. How can we tell that there is something to give attention to? I have a funny saying, "If you would be worried about a toddler exhibiting that behavior, you should probably be worried if your horse is doing it." This would include teeth grinding, jaw crossing, teeth tapping, grimacing (drawing the lips back from the incisors), gapping the mouth excessively, drawing the tongue behind the bit, putting the tongue over the bit, putting the tongue out the side of the mouth, and frenetic activity with the bit. Even bigger motions like head tossing, excessive pulling, refusing to take contact, and maintaining an over-flexed posture in the neck can be directly related to how the horse is interacting with the bit and the person at the other end of the reins.

The horse's mouth and tongue, almost parallel to our hands and fingers, are not only for eating but for expression and exploring. The horse's mouth and our hands have the most nerve density of our entire bodies. They are both have the greatest capability for delicate, complex, movements. They are truly the greatest tool of both horse and man with the most possibilities for complex and nuanced communication.

With the complex network rooted in the hyoid and the density of nerves in the mouth itself, the horse's mouth can become an area that suffers unnecessary and lasting trauma. Clearly, the best treatment is prevention through education.

4

The Horse's Neck

"To perform his business justly and gracefully, the animal must first be made supple in his fore parts; and his head and neck so managed, that one may be raised, and the other arched or bent to the hand to which he is to turn...For there is such an immediate and strict connection and dependency between the parts, that the change of posture in any single one, will affect the whole." ~de la Gueriniere (1688-1751)

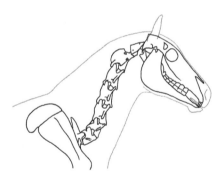

The neck undulates in the rhythm of the front legs reaching forward in the walk. The neck balances the movements of the canter. You have seen the horse that can balance with all four legs seeming to be in one place when the horse doesn't want to cross a ditch. The neck, in all its attitudes, makes the equine body function correctly. If the neck doesn't move in a healthy way, the rest of the body won't either.

As we try to create communication with a bit, we are by necessity, working through the neck. It is the most flexible area of the entire spine and boy is it flexible! That can make it difficult to maintain a fluid and consistent contact. This can result in the horse dropping the line of communication and changing his balance; maybe for the better but most likely for the worse.

Let's take some time to discuss the basic structure of the neck and how it functions. Having a basic knowledge of the workings of the neck can prevent us from using training methods that could do much more harm than good. (There are many resources if you would like to go deeper into anatomy and biomechanics.)

The 7 cervical vertebrae that make up the neck can each articulate along three planes: Longitudinal (up and down with flexion and extension), Lateral (side to side), and Axial (rotational as looking from the front or back). They can also work in any combination of the three.

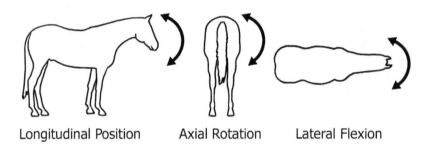

Longitudinal Position   Axial Rotation   Lateral Flexion

The muscles, tendons, and ligaments that articulate this complex structure are thickly layered across layers to protect the spinal column and are connected to the back, ribs, and belly muscles of the horse.

The neck and head comprise approximately 1/9 of the horse's entire weight. It is the structure through which the horse moves his head for his sensory organs to function at their best. Hearing, smelling, tasting, looking, and refined exploratory touching are all centered in the head facilitated by the neck.

With the neck, a horse reaches for food, lifts his head for a better view, and spars with a friend. The mechanics of the entire body are dependent on the neck for balance and counterbalance in all dimensions of movement.

Longitudinal Articulation

Extension of the Neck and Poll Flexion

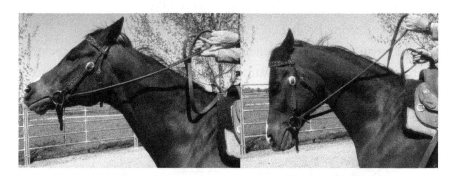

The horse can distinctly open or flex the poll joint, (the joint that connects the skull to the first cervical vertebra) opening the angle and closing it with lesser participation from the joints further down the neck. The extension and flexion of the poll are both important muscle movements. If all the horse knows is to flex the poll and has no idea of using the extensor muscles, instead of creating a positive contact for the horse to trust, the neck collapses behind the contact and any positive arc of communication is lost. The neck is in a posed position which creates tension and dysfunction of the neck that affects the entire body.

If the horse continues on this path and curls the neck overusing the joints in the mid-neck (think chin to chest) this is a physically and psychologically damaging position and should be avoided.

Lifting and Lowering

The horse can also move the entire neck higher and lower longitudinally. Maintaining contact (without punishment) if the neck "reverses," is part of the key to communicating to the horse where the healthier, more relaxed, more balanced neck position is. Many horses who "reverse" the neck are exhibiting anxiety, excitement, fear, resistance, or confusion. The result is that the muscles along the top of the neck and back are contracted and need to release and relax for the horse to be in a healthier posture. Trying to "fix" this with gadgets misses a key element: the forward and downward elongation of the neck instead of a backward and curled position which is not positive nor does it have a stretching or relaxing effect. The relaxation of the muscles throughout the neck and trunk is what creates a healthier posture.

The balance of the horse changes longitudinally forward as the neck stretches forward and downward. This is not a movement for creating balance to the hindquarters, it is a posture for relaxation and release.

LATERAL FLEXION

Lateral flexion is a useful movement for stretching and relaxing as well as shifting the balance of the horse on the lateral plane. The goal of lateral flexion is stretching the muscle structure of the neck on the convex side asking those muscle groups to relax while en-

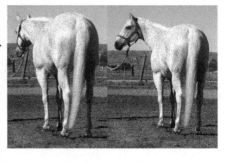

couraging the muscles on the concave side to aid in the flexion. Flexing on a single plane (laterally instead of twisting the neck) is a simpler request and can be a helpful gauge of the flexibility of the neck.

AXIAL ROTATION

Axial rotation of the neck is often described as twisting. Another description I've heard is "dropping an ear." Axial rotation is a bit more complex movement not seen expressed by itself very often. It can be a sign of tension if offered when asking for a lateral flexion or when simply working in hand. With muscles on both sides of the neck working, there can be a degree of isometric contraction (muscle contraction without actual motion) making relaxation of the major neck muscles difficult. It is something to be aware of when you are asking for a lateral flexion.

"We know that the head and neck play the role of a balancing pole, whose displacements simultaneously lead to the modification of the balance and movements of the trunk and legs." ~Jean Saint-Fort Paillard (1913-1990)

Along with the multiple flexion capacity of the equine neck, it also acts as both a balance and a counterbalance laterally and longitudinally. Changing the neck position can serve as a complement to support the balance or to change the balance when needed as it is 1/9 of the horse's total weight out in front of the shoulders.

What are the effects on the body when the neck changes position? Why is this important?

This was part of the focus of an experiment conducted in the 19th century by François Baucher and an equine science specialist, General Morris. To assess the effect of neck position on the longitudinal weighting of the fore and hind legs they went to the Paris customs office which contained two identical scales (assumed to be for weighing cattle). They placed the scales on a level surface, put the front legs of a mare they brought with them on the center of one scale and the hind legs on the center of the other. The mare was a bit heavy in the head and neck but otherwise common. She was fitted with both a saddle and bridle. Her total weight was 846 pounds.

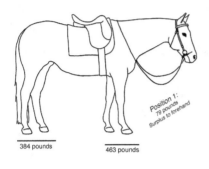

Position 1:
79 pounds
Surplus to forehand

384 pounds   463 pounds

As they asked the mare to place her neck in various positions, they notated the changes of weight from forehand to hindquarters. The first position was that of her choosing, relaxed with a fairly level neck. This could be seen as her personal neutral position according to her nature and conforma-tion.

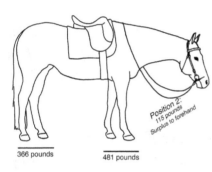

Position 2:
115 pounds
Surplus to forehand

366 pounds   481 pounds

In the second position they asked the mare to lower her neck but otherwise remain in the same position. Not surprisingly, 36 pounds shifted toward the fore-hand. The first observation must then be that lowering the neck puts weight toward the forehand.

The third position was raising the neck as high as was appropriate for the mare's conformation with-out asking for any other posture change. The above observation was confirmed as an 80-pound swing of weight shifted to the hindquarters.

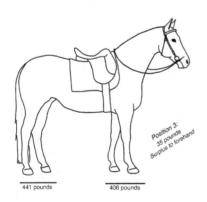

Position 3:
35 pounds
Surplus to forehand

441 pounds   406 pounds

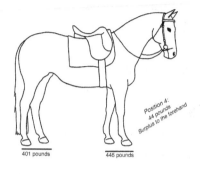

Position 4:
44 pounds
Surplus to the forehand

401 pounds   445 pounds

The fourth position was to ask the mare to flex the poll in the high position. Interestingly, the flexion of the poll slightly increased the weight to the forehand. This is an important detail to see because poll flexion is often seen as the ideal neck position in the horse. It needs to be noted that the horse's balance is affected by the difference between an open poll and poll flexion and not necessarily in a positive way for longitudinal balance.

For additional information on the effect of the rider's weight on the basic balance of the horse at a halt, Baucher mounted the mare.

Position 5:
119 pounds
Surplus to the forehand

434 pounds   553 pounds

With Baucher mounted, he allowed the mare to relax her neck, similar to the first position (position 5). By comparing the results to the results from the earlier first position, it was computed that of the riders total weight, 90 pounds weighed on the forehand and 23 pounds on the hindquarters.

Position 6:
40 pounds
Surplus to forehand

474 pounds   514 pounds

When Baucher leaned back slightly, raised the neck, and flexed the poll according to his method, an additional 40 pounds shifted to the hindquarters (position 6). Some of this was his own weight and most was the shifting weight of the change of neck position.

This experiment was repeated with another horse and returned very similar results. Undeniably the height of the neck directly affects the distribution of weight over the haunches and forehand of the horse. While the intricacies of movement, posture, and areas of tension can alter these results in motion, these facts remain:

- The ability to control the height of the neck offers some ability to longitudinally change the distribution of weight over the haunches and shoulders.
- In simple terms, a low neck draws more weight to the forehand. A higher neck shifts weight to the haunches.
- If our goal in riding is to have a balanced horse with greater amounts of weight shifted to the haunches, the low neck is counter-indicated.
- An extended neck, while not helpful for weight shift to the haunches, it does offer its own benefits for the overall well-being of the horse when used appropriately.

Baucher's conclusion seems to be scientifically accurate as well as thought-provoking. "Balance must be obtained without interference with movement while, on the other hand, movement in the act of being produced must not interfere with balance."

This isn't the only part of the picture of the neck as further study will uncover more nuanced muscle postures and usages that affect the balance of the horse longitudinally and laterally but it is a basic phenomenon we should be aware of. Using this information in an intelligent way in our education of the horse seems obvious as we allow or ask for various neck positions to help the horse fulfill our requests.

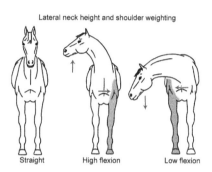

Lateral neck height and shoulder weighting

Straight   High flexion   Low flexion

The combination of lateral flexibility and the height of the neck gives us even more to consider. When the horse is in the position of lateral flexion, the neck can also be raised or lowered. In simplest terms (as horses are made of so many moving parts) a lateral flexion with a highly placed neck will likely encourage weighting of the shoulder on the opposite side of the flexion. A lateral flexion with a lower placement of the neck will likely encourage the increase of weight to the shoulder on the side of the flexion. In what way is this useful? To answer that, we must at least briefly consider the basic asymmetry of the horse.

"There are almost no perfectly straight horses. The horseman, with all the perfection of art, spends his life correcting this imperfection." ~Jacques d'Auvergne (1729-?)

This may seem obvious to those who have ridden any considerable length of time, however, I have observed that a clear understanding of this doesn't follow as closely as one would think. I've heard expressions like, "This is his good side/bad side," "He's stiff this way," "This is his hard way," and the like. What is missing is clarity on the basics of what is happening and some clear ways to counter it.

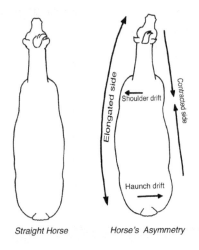

Elongated side

Shoulder drift

Contracted side

Haunch drift

Straight Horse   Horse's Asymmetry

If riding a horse straight or in alignment weren't such a challenge, I don't think d'Auvergne would have emphasized it so prominently. What are we talking about exactly? A straight horse could also be described as ambidextrous: equally flexible, strong, and balanced both to the left and to the right. Let's first consider the basic lateral asymmetry: The diagram serving as our sample "asymmetrical" horse has a natural tendency of incurvation to the right. The flexion of the neck to the right will be easier than the left because flexing to the left will require the stretching of the contracted muscles of the right side. By aligning the neck, the shoulders can become more aligned as well. When the horse naturally wants to flex to the right, the shoulders tend to drift to the left. You might notice when you ride a horse with this incurvation to the right, a circle gets bigger and bigger. When you ride them to the left, the circle gets smaller.

In the haunches, the drift will tend to be to the right as the horse is already positioned in the body to the right. The horse may struggle to pick up the left lead because of this.

A lot of problems can be solved if we understand even the most basic premises of the natural asymmetry of every horse. The flexion can be to the left or to the right but will likely have similar effects in the mirror image.

I know from riding a lot of horses that this part of the asymmetry is not the entire picture. There can also be misalignments and pathologic rotations of sections of the body just like in humans. For now, since we are focusing on the neck, contact, and interacting with the horse through the bit, this introduction to asymmetry should suffice. Another bit of bottom-line information: horses don't read the books. I've had some head-scratching situations that made no sense according to the manuals, but there they were. The best thing we can do is to try and understand the impact we can have on the elements of the body function we know about and keep our eyes open to more as we go.

"It is very clear that any constriction affecting the natural play of the neck muscles...necessarily leads to a corresponding constriction in the play of the horse's equilibrium and of its locomotive mechanism." ~Jean Saint-Fort Paillard

I don't feel I can pass through even a brief study on the neck as it relates to contact without discussing equipment, disciplines, and techniques that purposefully fix the neck in any one position. Without the appropriate movement of the neck, the back will cease to function correctly. This will cascade into the entire body. If the neck is forced into a low position, the horse is put into a position of having over 100 pounds shifted to the forehand before he even moves a muscle. If the neck is forced into a vertically flexed position without relaxation, again the gaits will be degraded from tension throughout the body. If the horse is brought behind the vertical and low (low, deep, round, etc) not only is 150 or more pounds shifted to the forehand, the horse's balance centers (vision and inner ear) are interrupted, and the nuchal ligament insertions can be damaged and torn. There is no place for this kind of restrictive and coercive ideology when we are striving for work that promotes and supports health in horses. It's long past time to put these detrimental "tools" away.

Stated simply: placing the horse's neck in a position contrary to the overall goal of healthy work is at the very least ineffectual, and could be considered cruel. Handicapping the horse from fulfilling our request is the antithesis of honor and respect due to the horse as his own sentient being.

The neck is the most flexible part of the horse's spine in all directions and can be carefully and intelligently used in lateral flexions and longitudinal position changes to stretch, strengthen, aid in balance, and relax the horse. With so many connections in the muscular, fascia, skeletal and nervous systems traveling through the neck, it can be an immensely powerful source of release throughout the body. Think about how you feel when your neck is stiff. It's distracting and uncomfortable. An adjustment can temporarily help, but isn't more positive, thorough, strengthening, stretching, and balancing of the neck muscles the best insurance of the stability of the spinal column? I believe this is the healthiest process for the horse and the most effective and efficient way to communicate with our horse.

AJSK Photography

"The horseman, therefore, should not act the part of a tyrant, but the part of a lover, not endeavour to force her submission, but strive to gain her consnet and good will, by assiduity, persevereance, and the gentlest attentions. For what prospect of success would rougher manners afford?" ~de la Gueriniere

5

A Bit about Bits

"*The famous Pignatel at Naples, never used but simple bits, which made the ignorant wonder how he could dress horses so perfectly with so few kinds of bits; but he freely told them, it was their ignorance made them wonder at his art: and likewise that great master of his art, Monsieur De Pluvinel, said the same.*"~ *William Cavendish Duke of Newcastle*

Since we are going to be working specifically with the education of the horse's mouth I thought it wise to offer some information about bits, identifying them and their effects. The main bit in question is the snaffle bit as it is used nearly exclusively for in-hand work with the horse.

Why would the snaffle be the bit of choice for the education of the mouth? It's simplicity. The effects of a snaffle used appropriately, are clear, painless, and direct. The action of the request through the bit is exactly what the horse receives unlike a bit with a shank. Shank bits alter the information in the horse's mouth via the leverage action and the chin strap. So the simple snaffle is the clearest tool for the job.

All too often I have a student go to the tack store to purchase a snaffle bit and become overwhelmed by the dizzying variety of choices in snaffle bits. I want to go over the basic snaffle bits and their differences.

Snaffle Bit Identification and Purpose

Snaffle bits are designed and identified by the cheek piece and the mouthpiece. The different combinations of mouthpieces and cheekpiece result in unique effects.

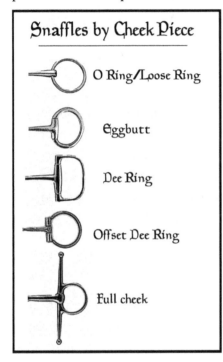

Snaffles by Cheek Piece

O Ring/Loose Ring

Eggbutt

Dee Ring

Offset Dee Ring

Full cheek

The simplest and most common snaffle is the Loose Ring. The ring moves freely through both ends of the mouthpiece, also called cannons. It is a versatile bit, used in both English and Western riding.

With the Eggbutt snaffle, the mouthpiece is fixed in place in relation to the cheekpiece. Some horses like it as the connection between the mouthpiece and cheekpiece is less abrupt.

The Dee ring snaffle (along with the Offset Dee and the Full Cheek) offers more support on the opposite side of the mouth from where the bit is being activated. If the bit is activated to the left, the cheek piece on the right comes in contact with the outside of the mouth on the right side supporting the request to the left. Or, as I was taught as a kid, "Keeps the bit from going through the mouth." Well, let's hope we aren't pulling that hard.

The Offset Dee ring is a western-style cheekpiece with a similar function; to support the rein aid on one side with pressure on the other. While not as much support as the regular Dee ring or the Full Cheek, it can be helpful especially to a western horse when they don't want to use the Full or Dee ring bits.

The Full Cheek gives the most support, especially on the offside of the flexion. Some horses like the extra effect and it can help particularly stabilize the horse in the contact laterally.

Other snaffle bits have different looks but few differing effects. I'm not going to address any gadgetry like slip gag or gag snaffles nor will I condone widespread use of twisted wire bits.

The various mouthpieces of snaffle bits have different functions but they can be considered a variation on a theme. The basics of the mouthpieces are less varied.

A Single Joint snaffle is exactly as it claims. The two pieces, called cannons, are joined together in the center of the mouthpiece via a joint that can be very mobile or limited in its mobility.

A Hollow Mouth snaffle (usually a single joint) is also as it says; instead of being solid metal, it is much larger in diameter and hollow in the cannons. Horses that are shy about receiving contact often do better in a hollow mouth. The larger the diameter of the cannon, the milder the bit because there is more surface area in contact with the tongue and lips. Inversely, the narrower the bit in diameter, the harsher it is. A Hollow Mouth can be 23mm in diameter compared to regular mouthpieces that vary from 12mm-18mm. Bradoon snaffles (used in conjunction with a Weymouth curb for a double bridle in dressage) can be as small as 10mm to keep the mouth from being overly crowded with metal from the two bits.

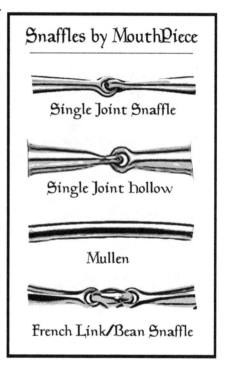

Snaffles by MouthPiece

Single Joint Snaffle

Single Joint hollow

Mullen

French Link/Bean Snaffle

A Mullen Snaffle is simply a straight or curved bar. A few have a low port in them. It is a very good tool for horses that are too active with bits that can articulate like a regular or French link, horses that are extremely shy about receiving contact, or horses that need even less complicated communication than a Single Joint Snaffle. I have had wonderful results from using the mullen in these situations because of its very "boring" feel to the horse. It doesn't move, it doesn't articulate, the action is the same without any angle changes...boring. Some horses need this for a time.

French Link, Bean Snaffle. The French Link, not particularly French in its origin, is a snaffle bit with two joints. The cannons are connected to a "Bean" (because of the shape) in the middle. Today the bit is touted as "tongue relief" but it isn't necessary to provide tongue relief if you are not acting directly on the tongue with the bit. There are horses that like the mobility of a French link as well as the angle it creates on the corners of the lips (where we would prefer the pressure to be). This bit is, to me, more of a preference of the horse. Some really like it, some don't, some don't care.

Many bits with shanks can also be solid, two pieces, three pieces, or more. Bitting is a very old study and practice. Bitting and mouthpiece design can be found in treatises on equitation as early as mid 16th Century Italy. This engraving (above left) details an entire shop devoted to the creation of the correct bit for each individual horse. It was written by Cesare Fiaschi.

Along with cheekpieces and mouthpieces, there is the metal that the mouthpiece is made of. The most common substance is stainless steel. Rumor has it (because I don't spend time licking mouthpieces of horses) that the metals taste and feel different to the horses. I can say, from 40 years of experience, a lot of horses and a lot of bridles, horses do have preferences.

Stainless seems to be quite neutral. If you think about it, we eat off of stainless steel silverware most of the time, and the flavor of the food isn't carried in the utensils. That's why we use them (plus they are durable and don't rust).

Copper is popular as it is said to cause salivation. Some horses like it and it does seem to bring about a wetter mouth. I've had horses that simply wouldn't tolerate it. Perhaps the flavor and experience are simply too strong for them. Other copper blends are used to encourage salivation like copper with a small percentage of zinc and or manganese.

The bit material I've found that has the most universal acceptance is sweet iron. Sweet iron is cold-rolled "mild steel" (also referred to as carbon steel, black steel, blue steel.) Sweet iron will release sweet-tasting surface rust through contact with saliva. I came to sweet iron bits through the western world I grew up in but have continued using them because I haven't had a horse who was put off by a sweet iron mouthpiece. Another carbon iron combination (steel is an alloy of carbon and iron) is cast iron. Many people, including me, prefer the taste of food cooked on cast iron for the flavor retention ability. It imbues a bit of dietary iron into the food as well as the flavor of what was previously cooked making the taste of food richer and more complex. I believe that sweet iron bits do this for horses to an extent as well.

Other materials that can be used as mouthpieces or as a supplement to mouthpieces are differing plastics, leather, leather wrap, latex wrap, even rope of differing kinds. These can be helpful for horses' recovery from trauma in the contact or horses who have issues in the mouth (damage to the tongue, damage to the bars, large tongue, low palate, drawn back tongue, tongue out the side of the mouth). I've found plastic mullen bits the most beneficial for this process.

I have some further comments on some other kinds of "snaffle" bits. Some are not technically true snaffles and some incorrectly claim a mild effect.

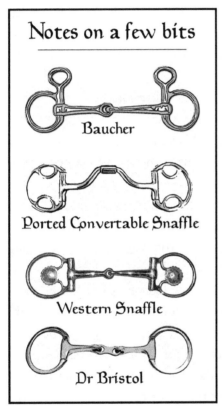

Notes on a few bits

Baucher

Ported Convertable Snaffle

Western Snaffle

Dr Bristol

At the top of the diagram is a Baucher snaffle. There is no real evidence linking this bit to Francois Baucher (1796-1873) or his work. The mouthpiece can be any of the options: single joint, French link, or mullen but it is the way the bit connects to the bridle (called a hanging cheek) that gives it a more indirect effect on the horse. That's why, if you want to get really picky, this may not be a true snaffle in the sense of having only a direct effect on the tongue and lips. There is an indirect, slight rotational effect when the reins activate this bit. The horse either likes dislikes or doesn't care about the effect. When doing in-hand work, I do not like the Baucher cheekpiece because of the indirect effect as well as the small rings of the cheekpiece. It is difficult to remain clear from the ground and while teaching the aids. I don't discourage the use of the bit, it's simply awkward to use for this purpose.

The second bit, Ported Convertable Snaffle is a lot of things actually. It can function as a ported mullen when used with the reins in the snaffle position on the cheekpiece. It can function as a correctional mouthpiece encouraging poll flexion if the rein is set in the lower ring instead of in the snaffle position. For the education of the mouth, this bit is too complicated and has too much happening to be clear. I don't want a bit requesting things based on the design, like poll flexion. If I want poll flexion, I want to have a specific aid to ask for poll flexion, not lift the rein and the bit does it for me. The inner rings on the cheek pieces also limit how I can work with my hands with this bit.

The Western Snaffle has an offset Dee cheekpiece and is a perfectly fine bit to use except for the ornamentation on the inside of the rings. I can't get my thumb or my fingers inside the ring to work easily with the horse.

The Dr. Bristol can be confused with a French link but they have a VERY important difference: the link is flat instead of bean-shaped. The flat "dogbone" link has a much more severe impact on the tongue than the bean, which is the same diameter as the cannons of the bit. The flat link of the dogbone has an edge that the horses can feel making it quite a strong bit usually used for control. I don't want the intensity of my aids increased simply from the design of my mouthpiece. I don't use Dr. Bristol bits and don't recommend them.

Let's return to the idea of salivation and a wet mouth. What is the big deal about the horse salivating? What is a dry mouth or a wet mouth and why does it even matter? Several reasons, actually, and they may not be the reasons you think. The relaxed movement of the mouth is talked about in the earliest treatises, The Rules of Riding by Grisone published in Naples in 1550, "…with a gentle support, he will establish a connection between the bridle and his [the horse's] mouth, chewing it always so that it will look at if it [the bit] were miraculously born inside [the horse's mouth.]" "Chewing" may be one description but later writings clarify a "murmuring," "savoring" (like hard candy) type of movement. It is this kind of movement that, in the French tradition is referred to as *session de machoire* or release of the jaw. In a full release, the horse feels and moves the bit in his mouth activating the salivary gland, and then swallows. This is the cycle that is being sought because it is part of the autonomic nervous system and indicates (usually) a released jaw and relaxed state of mind.

Don't be fooled, however, by a horse that is slobbering. The full cession de machoir includes *swallowing*. If the horse doesn't swallow but drools, you could compare that to a person who has a hard candy in their mouth and drools instead of swallowing. Something is definitely wrong! Just as a relaxed movement of the jaw and tongue of a horse activates the salivary  gland, the natural result should be swallowing! Without swallowing there is still tension in the system. Releasing the tension in the most innervated area of the horse is simply a brilliant focus to promote relaxation in the entire horse. Leave it to men of centuries past staking their very lives on their horses and horsemanship to notice the details that make the greatest impact.

Horses are individual and the amount of saliva they produce from their three salivary glands can add up to ten gallons per day! Saliva is the perfect pH balancer of the stomach and if the pH in the stomach is good, they are less likely to develop ulcers. So an additional benefit to the release of the jaw is a more positive pH balance in the stomach.

The reason people say they want the horse to have a moist mouth is that it is more comfortable to move the bit around and they are relaxed. Maybe. I don't think that the horse above right is an example of relaxation. As in many things, look deeper at the horse and ask yourself honestly if he is relaxed, moving his mouth nonchalantly, picking up and dropping the bit quietly with his tongue...then you find a bit of saliva wetting the lips. It's not the slobber that proves anything. It's the quality of relaxation in the movement of the tongue and jaw. The "lipstick" is simply the result.

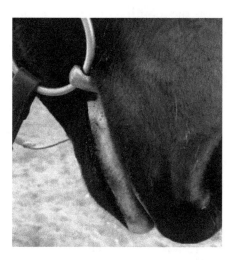

Is the Snaffle really a Good Bit?

A common concern I hear from riders about snaffles is the "nut-cracker effect" they see in the snaffle bit use and design. Another concern is the pressure that the snaffle can put on the tongue. These are both easily answered and effectively eliminated by the upward action of the hand in place of a backward or downward action. This has been the practice of the use of the aid of the hand for centuries. From Francois de la Gueriniere to Francois Baucher, the description of the action of the hands is lifting the hand keeping the elbow close to the body (or as low as you can) while turning the fingernails upward. With this action, the bit acts primarily on the corners of the mouth and not the tongue or the bars. Here are some diagrams to help explain the reasoning behind the lifting hand.

This horse's head is in an open neutral position and the bit is sitting in the mouth without any indications from the rein. The horse can adjust the bit to his liking with the tongue and the tongue can move freely under the bit.

The bit is lifted by the rider into the corners of the lips. Little pressure is exerted on the tongue, the bars, or the roof of the mouth. The aid is clear, however, because the bit changes position in the mouth while still allowing full freedom to the tongue for relaxation. The horse feels free to reach into the con-

tact as it is comfortable to do so and the rider can ask for flexion, raising the neck, lowering the neck, and change of gaits without limiting the relaxation and mobility in the mouth.

The bit is pulled with a low hand putting more pressure on the tongue and bars. The only way for the horse to alleviate the pressure is with poll flexion or taking the chin toward the chest. This has the horse evade the pressure instead of being willing to move with it. There is no reason to follow this pres-

sure as it only leads the horse one way: backward. The trust of the hand is diminished because of the trapping of the tongue (it can no longer move freely under the bit). Horses will often draw their tongue back, put the tongue over the bit or out the side of the mouth to avoid this discomfort.

As the horse flexes the poll, we see an even more severe effect of the pulling effect on the horse's tongue and now the bars and the palate. The tongue is extremely compressed and the extremely sensitive bars are also being affected.

Same poll flexion with a lifted hand position. Again, the bit articulates, which the horse can feel on his tongue, but without pressing on the tongue, bars, or palate. The snaffle moves up and down on the tongue which is still free to move and keeps full blood flow and innervation which is impeded by the low, pulling hand.

The work in the real world is transformational. Communication can happen without force and with greater indication and clarity of the request. I don't ride with my hands in the air all the time, I simply, like the old masters, lift my hand for requests instead of pull. When the request is complete, the hand/arm can relax into the traditional elbow-hand-mouth position. I am demonstrating this on Minnie. In the first photo, I am requesting a flexion so I lift my hands leaving my elbows near my ribs. In the second photo, I have no current requests so my hands are in descent de main or discontinuing their action.

In the close-up photos, you can see more clearly how I lift the hands for my request and return them to the neutral position. The white arrow indicates where the pressure on the horse's tongue would increase exponentially if a low hand was used to indicate requests. With the lifting hand instead of the pulling hand, we can create an amazing, cooperative relationship between the hand and the horse's mouth through the tool of a snaffle bit.

A Bit about Nosebands

You may have noticed the lack of cavessons or nosebands in the photographs in this book. There is a reason for that. I am reticent to muzzle the horses in their expressions or limit the mobility of the mouth and jaw.

Research is already revealing the damaging effect of overtight nosebands on the nasal bones and the nerves of the horse's face. Even a noseband that you can put two fingers under can be restricting the articulation the horse needs to activate his autonomic nervous system, mobilize his tongue and swallow.

Without that, the horse's systems are working to overcome this limitation. This can cause stress, depression, and ulcers in horses.

Even placing extra padding under the noseband doesn't make it kinder. It actually makes it more restrictive. For extra padding to stay under the noseband, the noseband has to be cranked even tighter. Nowadays, it is even difficult to find a simple noseband without a crank (to add leverage to make the noseband tighter).

The noseband as it is used now is a young piece of equipment. In the early treatises on horsemanship, the noseband was merely an afterthought. It was used in Guerinier's work as a means to ask for lateral flexion while riding with a curb. The cavesson was not used only to close the horse's mouth.

If the horse is struggling in the mouth by gaping, putting the tongue over the bit, or out the side of the mouth, there is a deeper problem. Ask the question, "Why is the horse responding so poorly to the rein aids?" Then review how the rein aids are being used.

With a clear understanding of bits and the effect on the horse's entire body via the mouth, we can choose our actions more wisely. We can make better use of each request. We can be more clear in our requests and best of all, the horse has a space to participate instead of simply reacting. The question is not how we can create a bit that will help alleviate pressure on the tongue, it's how we can work in such a way that we don't put painful pressure on the tongue in the first place.

6

Getting Started In-Hand

"An old rusty lock is stubborn and difficult to open. After many fruitless attempts, we are likely to grow impatient and try to force it. We waste our time and energy and end up twisting or breaking the key with the lock still unopened. Suppose, on the contrary, we send for a locksmith: he gently takes the key and with no effort-presto!-the lock clicks open. Here we have the action of the hands."
~Etienne Beaudant 1863-1949

We have discussed in some length the human hand, the equine mouth and neck. We've concluded clearly that the mouth is delicate and intertwined with the entire body of the horse. The clearest and simplest way to educate the hand and the horse's mouth is through bit work undertaken  from the ground. The first author to mention work with the bit on the ground is Italian Claudio Corte in his work *Il cavallarizzo (The Horseman)* first published in 1562. It's definitely not a recent fad!

When we work from the ground we can see what our hand is doing and the horse's responses to the bit and its movement. We can see even the smallest changes the horse makes. We can clearly feel what the mouth and tongue are doing because we are interacting with the bit directly with our fingers instead of through the intermediary of the reins. We can be grounded and stationary, easier for the horse to relate to, and easier for us to be stable in our torso and arms if the horse moves in opposition to our request. From their back, we are moving with them (which can be beneficial for some things but makes the understanding of the relationship between hand and mouth more complicated). We have our hands close by the mouth to be able to support the bit request with clarification if needed. A touch here, lift there can make the difference between understanding and resistance. We can teach and refine the actions of the hands before we even get on the horse. In fact, by working with the bit from the ground, the horse has only one focus (the bit) instead of several: the changing weight of the rider, the rider's legs, coordination of his own movement with the rider aboard, voice commands, and whip aids to mention a few.

I would be remiss if I failed to mention the extensive benefits of in-hand work for not only the education of horses but also for the rehabilitation of horses with trouble in the contact, young horses beginning their work, and carriage driving equine of all sizes. Any horse that works with a bit (and even a cavesson) can benefit from this work.

"Many riders don't understand that the lack of intelligence, the rudeness, and the coarseness of their hands aggravate their horses or make them lose their balance." Jean-Claude Racinet (1929-2009)

Racinet may seem to be stating his case in strong language but what he is saying is still true. It is as clear as can be that the education of our hands is crucial to our horsemanship journey. With educated hands, the education of the horse's mouth can begin in earnest.

Looking back on the written work of Baucher, Fillis, Bussigny, Froissard, Racinet, DeCarpentry, and Karl, we can see a variety of applications of work in-hand as it relates to the education of the horse's mouth. Some who work in-hand, hold the reins a few inches from the bit while others hold the reins near the buckle. Some hold both reins in one hand close to the bit or farther back. Some only ask for flexions in the halt while others find flexions useless unless the horse is walking. Some ask for flexion of the poll early in the education while others wait for poll flexion until the end of their program. These ecuyers educated in the French tradition lived in different time periods, studied under different masters, and interacted with different horses. When we look at their work from a bigger picture view, what stands out as obvious is a cumulative, broad experience that reaches back some 200 years. It is just as applicable today as it has ever been when we add our new understanding of ethology and the complex systems of the horse.

"It cannot be expected that he [a young colt] will be guided, and go with ease to himself or pleasure to the rider, if the instrument by which he is to be conducted offends, or gives him pain: all habits and acquirements should be attained gradually, and almost imperceptibly."
~François de la Guérinière (1688-1751)

With a green or young horse, you can introduce these flexions in a halter or a cavesson to accustom the horse to moving with the hand both mentally and physically. Afterward, you can move them into the bit for the flexions. When I do introduce the bit, I allow them to wear it while I am doing groundwork and lunging in a halter or cavesson.

I start with in-hand work in the halt from a position in front of the horse. From this position, I have the closest interaction with the bit and his mouth and I can support him much more with parts of my hand on his head if he needs it. This can be invaluable if a horse is really struggling with the bit or any of the requests. A little support can go a long way!

From the time I set my eyes on the horse, I am observing how they are interacting with both me and the bit at the beginning of each session. It's also how I observe a horse I don't know and begin the conversation.

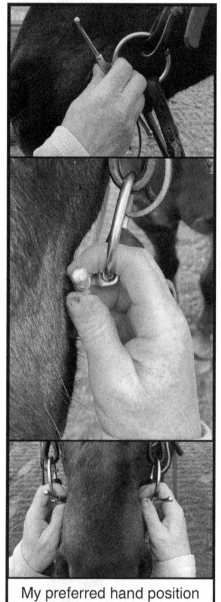

My preferred hand position

The in-hand work begins in a snaffle because the actions are direct, without leverage thus much more simple than with other bits. The snaffle can be solid (mullen), single joint, or have two joints with a bean in between. I like the bean to be quite small so the joints of the bit are not over the bars of the lower jaw causing possible insult to the bars themselves. Loose ring, D ring, full cheek, egg-butt, or Fullmer are all suitable for the work.

There are several different handholds that work well for differing situations while working in the halt from the front of the horse. My preference is with my thumb and fingers on the mouthpiece itself. The thumb through the ring of the bit or even holding onto the reins can all offer positive results. The reason I hold the mouthpiece is that I can closely feel the movements of the tongue and jaw.

The first thing I am looking for is what kind of response will the horse offer if I quietly lift the bit, more or less, toward the ears. Will the horse move the bit around softly in the mouth or will he offer some form of confusion or tension? Perhaps he will offer nothing at all, remaining stoic and mute. Another response is to fix his mouth and neck against any form of movement, even pushing back toward my hand. "Interesting," I say to myself. Then the conversation begins in earnest. "What is it?" I ask again and again. "What are you trying to tell me?" Little by little I peel away superfluous or contrary reactions until we reach a base level of understanding: my hands and the bit are here to talk, not to demand, invoke fear, or needlessly dominate. I know the horse has heard when he can stay with me in my hand, finding where the bit is comfortable in the mouth, and gently, in relaxation, move the bit in the mouth.

It may seem petty or excessive to spend so much time and focus on the horse's reaction to the bit. In fact, when I first began learning the work in hand, I did so with a shrug. "It can't hurt." I thought to myself. The more I learned through observing the work with increasing numbers of horses, the more I realized that a relaxed mouth is a relaxed horse. It's the "key" spoken of for the "lock" from the quote at the beginning of this chapter. I encourage you to be patient, keep trying, keep observing and find an instructor familiar with this methodology. (There are not many but they are out there.)

Another hand position

Once I feel the horse can receive some input in quietness, I ask them a simple request: perhaps to lift the neck if they feel heavy or to flex the neck laterally if they feel stiff. More questions arise and more observations are made. Is it hard for the horse to respond to my suggestion? Can he not flex at all or lift the neck? If so, then the trouble, as are all troubles, mental, emotional, and physical in varying degrees.

Physically, we see horses often flick a fly off their shoulder or torso with their nose and scratch many places on their bodies with their teeth. If they struggle greatly to offer even a minimum flexion, it could very well be physical, (arthritis or old injury to the neck). Even so, we can't write off the mental or emotional, especially when we are dealing with the mouth.

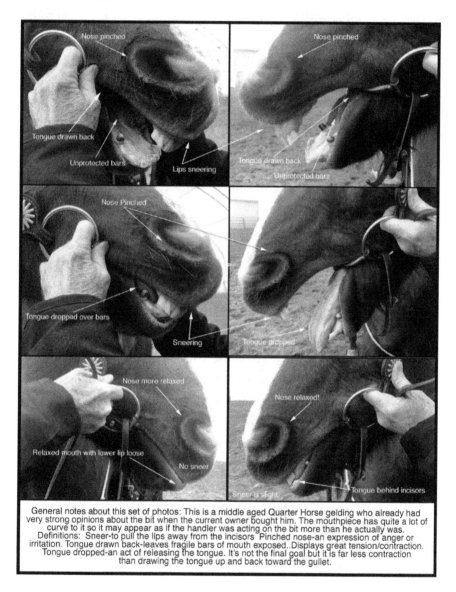

General notes about this set of photos: This is a middle aged Quarter Horse gelding who already had very strong opinions about the bit when the current owner bought him. The mouthpiece has quite a lot of curve to it so it may appear as if the handler was acting on the bit more than he actually was. Definitions: Sneer-to pull the lips away from the incisors Pinched nose-an expression of anger or irritation. Tongue drawn back-leaves fragile bars of mouth exposed..Displays great tension/contraction. Tongue dropped-an act of releasing the tongue. It's not the final goal but it is far less contraction than drawing the tongue up and back toward the gullet.

Mentally, the horse may simply not understand a different request than he has been asked for before. He may think he knows the answer and offers something you didn't ask for, like taking his chin toward his chest or avoiding the contact altogether. He may be distracted or find the whole situation boring or bothersome. The solution is to be as clear as possible with the requests while paying close attention to his responses. We are at the information-gathering stage.

The emotional side can complicate the investigation even further. This can be a tangle to tweeze apart with horses that have had negative experiences with the bit. Pain in the mouth is unlike pain anywhere else as we can understand. If you had a toothache, you would not be enthusiastic about food regardless of how delicious it might be. Your attitude toward food would become very poor, even fearful, resentful, ridden with anxiety, or even outbursts of anger.

"The aim of the wise is not to secure pleasure, but to avoid pain."
~Aristotle

We commonly have a situation where we are trying to educate the horse about the very place in his body that he fears being hurt. This is a slow process that must have clarity and patience to regain the horse's confidence that the bit will not cause pain or confusion. Some say to take the bit away entirely and simply circumvent the problem. It's a choice you can make for sure, but I will present the idea of playing the violin with your wrists instead of your fingers. It can be done, but is it the best tool for the job? IF we are up to taking on the task of educating our hands to the level that the horse needs to feel safe in his mouth, then the mouth is, by far, the superior location for extremely subtle communication. If we are not up to the task, bitless may be the way to go to save the horse a lot of pain, frustration, and anxiety. Working bitless should, in no way, be an abandonment of the education of the hand, simply a change of tools.

A critical element to the earliest education of the horse's mouth, both under saddle and in hand, is the idea of the hand following the mouth until the horse can learn to follow the hand. By maintaining contact with the mouth as the uneducated horse tries different ideas, the horse has the opportunity to learn that the contact is painless and consistent. It's like the child who tries all kinds of ideas to avoid eating the broccoli but learns that it is staying on the plate until he eats it. No force, no punishment, just following with the same contact. It's not a complicated idea but that doesn't mean it's an easy thing to accomplish! That mouth can go a lot of places! We need to be really flexible in all the joints of our fingers, wrists, and elbows to keep the same connection until the horse understands. When is the best time to follow the mouth and when do we begin to have the mouth follow the hand? That comes from instruction and experience.

Iris is missing an eye and the end of her tongue
Her education continues in a simple hackamore

Back to creating stability and understanding in the mouth. The goal is to work toward an agreement between your hand (via the bit) and the horse's position with a relaxed mouth and jaw. Regardless of where you move the bit (flexing him laterally, asking for his neck to be higher or lower, etc), he learns how to find the comfortable spot, (in agreement with the bit) and release his jaw with easy movements. How do we get there?

In simplest terms, we use the actions of the hands that fit the situation best. A way of categorizing the possibilities is Request, Reprieve, Resist, Release.

Actions
of the hand

Request
Reprieve
Resist
Release

Request-to ask for politely. The means of acting will be in respect of the horse's mouth so it will involve movements that lift the bit in the mouth instead of pulling back or down. Requests in the reins can include lateral flexions, extending the neck, demi arret (repeated upward actions of the hands to open the poll, lift the neck, or lighten the contact).

Reprieve-a postponement from expected consequences. The length of the reprieve is up to the horse. This ceasing of the aids of the hand is called descente de main (stop acting, offer a lighter connection in the reins while still maintaining informative contact). Descente de main can be a lowering of the hand slightly. It can also be the softening of the fingers. Informative contact is that which you can still feel his mouth and what is happening there but with, perhaps, a more supple contact. This is where the horse learns that he can remain connected while learning to carry out the request on his own at first for just moments, then longer and longer. This is the road to self-carriage in the hand. By maintaining a light contact, the connection isn't broken therefore it doesn't need to be reestablished to offer another request.

Resist-withstand the action or effect of. Resisting can be expressed on a scale. On one end a gentle resistance to communicate to a horse that the movement he is offering is not desired can be a simple delay in following the horse's ideas. On the farthest end of that spectrum is holding the bit quite firmly in one place while the horse offers unwanted responses until the horse realizes that comfort is found when he seeks out where the bit is. Sometimes this is the clearest procedure so that the horse doesn't have a moving target. Other times a slight resistance is all they need and full resistance would only upset the horse.

Resisting in one rein at a time is a tool of teaching primarily poll flexion later in the education of the hand. Resisting in one hand can also be an alternative way to explain a flexion resistance issue that the horse needs to sort for himself.

Release-Set free. When a horse fulfills the request to the desired end, he can be set free or put on the buckle. The release can be at any gait or at the halt for as little or as much time as will benefit the horse. This may not be an action, per se, but it is a decision-based in the aids that affect the horse in reference to the bit.

An example of how these actions might look like in use: I Request through a demi arret that my horse lighten the contact in the bit as I work with him in hand from the front. When he lifts his head a bit, he earns a Reprieve. He lowers his head again becom-

The direction of the demi arret

ing heavy in the contact so I once more Request via demi arret. He earns the Reprieve once more and I Release by removing my hands from the bit as an end to that portion of the conversation.

When I pick up the bit again after the Release, his mind will be refreshed for a new conversation. The release is also a way to reward him for participating well. This chain of actions of the hand then can be described Request (lighten your contact please using demi arret), Reprieve (He has lightened by slightly lifting his head so I utilize descente de main), Request (he has become heavy again so I request lightness once more through demi arret). Reprieve (descente de main because of his good response again). Release (by taking my hands off of the bit and giving him freedom).

The use of a Reprieve instead of a full Release is to grow the interconnectedness and consistency of the communication through the hand. Any time the contact with the bit or reins is released, the connection is interrupted. When the contact is picked up again, the connection takes a moment to become established again. Why go through this when we can be much more clear with infinitely smaller, more exacting aids in the hand? I do admit that developing this ability takes time, education, and conscientious effort. If we're spending the time riding anyway, why not develop our abilities?

The action of Resisting is used in accordance with the need for clarification in the horse taking his personal traits and current circumstances into consideration. Even in the early stages of the conversation in hand, Resisting the horse's actions can be helpful. What might Resisting look like in hand? I quietly pick up the contact from the front and the horse begins to toss his head. I begin to Resist, at first lightly and with increasing steadiness or weightiness until the horse discovers that his head tossing is gaining him nothing positive. Upon his steadying his head in the contact, I will   Reprieve for a moment then Release. This set of actions ended up being Request (the contact), Resist (to discourage the head tossing), Reprieve (when he's steady or steadier), Release (to reward him and allow him time to think.) The exploration of these actions will continue in the work under saddle.

> *"In equitation, we obtain much by requiring only a little at a time."*
> *~James Fillis*

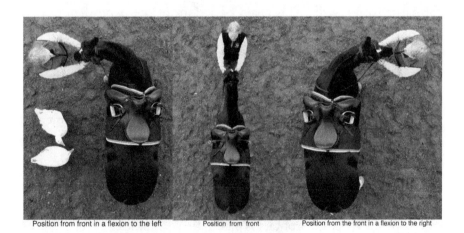

Position from front in a flexion to the left   Position from front   Position from the front in a flexion to the right

Once the mouth is fairly quiet and relaxed, I will make a request based on my observations. The first two I would most likely choose from is a demi arret to see if the horse will easily lift his head a bit to lighten the contact or a lateral flexion to evaluate the horse's lateral flexibility. Most often I begin with a light demi arret, a repeating action toward the crown of the bridle. Once I feel the horse's willingness to "carry his own head," then I will likely move on to the lateral flexion.

My request for the lateral flexion is enacted by leading with the hand on the side I am flexing toward and supporting with the hand on the other side. Not only am I learning about the horse's understanding of following the hand, but I can also evaluate the flexibility of the neck. I will ask for as much flexion as the horse can offer while keeping his head straight up and down. The goal is a smooth following of the request from straight to lateral flexion either way while the horse maintains the same height in the neck. As you can see from the photos from the ground, my mare Kali has her head at the same height while her neck is straight and in both flexions. This is also the seeds of creating some of the tools we will need to help the horse's asymmetry.

Once we have worked our way patiently through the reactions of the horse to the bit and its sensations. Our horse can maintain a relaxed mouth and tongue and accepts the bit as part of the communication system. Tension in the mouth and neck have been worked through and the horse is free of anxiety. With the support of hands on either side of the bit, the horse can lift the head and neck and flex the neck up to 90 degrees in both directions while maintaining a steady connection and height. Believe it or not, we have accomplished a lot. This is already a fantastic foundation for us to build on.

AJSK Photography

7

In-Hand From the Side

     "It takes a long and varied experience to know a horse's
mouth; to appreciate its delicate sensibilities when gently
manipulated in contrast with its extreme resistance when
force is roughly attempted." ~Etienne Beudant (1863-1949)

We will continue to educate the mouth and stretch the horse's neck laterally and longitudinally as he is able physically, mentally, and emotionally. We need no more than 90 degrees laterally. That is plenty to stretch the muscles in the neck, base of the neck, and into the torso. We will also teach the horse to lengthen the neck

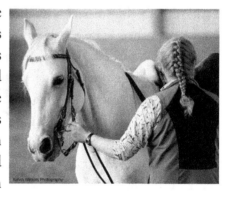

reaching forward and downward for balance change, clarity in the contact, and relaxation. It will also become clear to the horse how to follow the hand coordinating the contraction and relaxation of groups of muscles in order to perform the flexion or lengthening. Then he has experience receiving the requests from the bit in a relaxed manner.

Before moving to work from the side, the horse should have a gently mobile mouth, relaxed jaw and demeanor while in light contact with the bit. He can articulate the flexions while we guide him from the position in front of him. Then we can continue the educational process.

We are most able to support and teach from the front. From the side, we are coming closer to replicating what the actions would feel from the saddle or in some cases, from a carriage.

Start here   Two fingers in the bit ring with the rein in my hand   Close my hand with my thumb over the cheek piece

I use a standard working position when I am doing flexions from the side or working in the walk. I've seen other handholds both in person and in print or video. Instead of holding the bit, they might hold the rein a few inches from the bit. Some ecuyers hold both reins in one hand near the bit, others near the buckle. Some do only work at the halt while others state that without movement, flexions are useless. I will show you what has been working for me.

Starting from the left side of the horse, we use the left hand at the ring of the bit. The right hand holds the right rein from the offside of the bit passed over the base of the neck. The right hand settles in its position on the meat of the shoulder. Try to stand equidistant between both of your

Position of the rear hand holding the offside rein

hands for the most efficient work. The action of the front hand is up toward the ears. The action of the rear hand is down toward the ground (which lifts the bit on the opposite side of the neck).

As we did from the front, I want to check that the horse is relaxed before moving on to any flexions. One way to check his basic equilibrium is the light demi-arret in the left hand when standing on the left. Is the horse in a basic balance enough to offer the feeling that he is "carrying his own head?" Don't forget that a lower neck tends to bring weight to the shoulders and a higher neck tends to shift weight to the haunches. Is he heavy over his shoulders and in your hand or is his balance such that his head and neck are buoyant? If not, continue to use the demi-arret until you attain the feeling that he is carrying his own head and neck. Now come the flexions of the horse while working from the side.

Positions for the flexions away from me

The first flexion I prefer to do is a flexion away from me. This is the easiest for me to support the horse as he's learning. In the flexion away from me, I can better manage any axial rotation of the neck (twisting) much more effectively. Unwanted axial rotation can cause tension so I try to correct this as much as I can.

The Request for the flexion away from me is drawing down with my rear hand asking for the flexion toward the offside. I support and follow, even push slightly, if needed, to attain the bend the horse is comfortable with. Now the horse is receiving input in the mouth from a place closer to where we will be under saddle. If he responds well, we pause in Reprieve. If the horse fusses in the Request, I do my best to follow him at first to maintain the contact. As we work together, I will follow less and be more steady in my guidance. I stay with his mouth until he can stay with my hand.

Alternate lateral flexion away. The lifted rein can prevent unwanted axial rotation

If the confusion continues and the horse struggles by offering various movements including tossing, shaking, diving, or pushing, I need to check in with the horse and do my best to discern any physical or emotional sources for the behavior. If I have done my work from the front thoroughly, the work from the side shouldn't be a big leap of understanding. If there is some trouble, this is one of those many moments where I must be as fair and objective as possible. I must remember that I am working in his mouth. I have some choices here: I could go back to repeat the work from the front to clarify and return to the flexions from the side. I could also stay in the work from the side and try some adjustments and see if comprehension improves. The decision is based in what I perceive from the horse throughout the process.

The trouble could be caused by many things from timidity and fear to boredom and learned pushiness. These situations call for internal and external stability. Timidity brings supple support from me. Learned pushiness would bring rooted firmness. These evaluations and responses will be repeated throughout the education of the horse.

Back to the flexion. As he moves his neck I want to stay equally between my hands so I step around as he flexes. I can be stable, supportive, and clear. After attaining an appropriate amount of flexion I will pause while maintaining the contact. I want the horse to begin the process of learning to wait. A flexion later may be needed in a movement under saddle and if he isn't clear about maintaining flexion of the neck, I have too much to manage. The more the horse can learn to maintain, the less I have to remind him of.

Pausing at the end of the flexion also allows me to see if he is participating by relaxing the stretching muscles and activating the muscles that are helping create the flexion. We want the work to positively affect both sides of the body. We are stretching and strengthening, much like yoga.

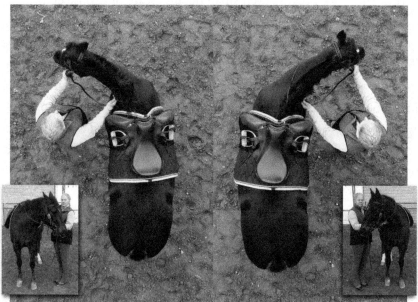

Positions for the flexions toward me

Once the horse is quite proficient at this flexion, following the rein request from over the neck without twisting, then I feel much more confident that we can ask for the flexion toward us. With only the inside rein to guide him, there is much less support for correcting any dropping of the head and neck or twisting.

Flexing toward me, per the Code, involves lifting up on the left ring of the bit (when flexing toward me) and drawing it slightly toward me. While doing this, I soften the offside rein (in this case, the right rein) while keeping light contact. This allows for flexion without creating conflicting input from me.

At this point, the horse is usually becoming comfortable with the process and we can add some specifics that will reap benefits later. One detail is that we want the neck height to stay the same throughout the flexions. Whatever height you have chosen to begin the flexions (usually at a height where he isn't leaning), stay on a horizontal plane while performing the flexions. We would like to separate and clarify each part of the work because even small details create or expose emotional, mental, or balance changes. If the horse drops or raises the head, pushes into the bit, or makes any other changes, take a break and repeat the flexions again. We are looking for deep clarity here while we build the foundation of understanding of the aids felt in the mouth. Once again, I'm looking toward a consistent height and contact. The complete agreement between the horse and me. Yes, this does take time, patience, and stability. But if we can't create the understanding from the ground, how will we create it any better from the back?

Changing the Height of the Neck: Lift and Lengthen

I have mentioned neck height already as one means of changing the overall balance of the horse. The height of the neck, depending on the muscles that are at play, can help with changing balance, stretching, and relaxation. This is

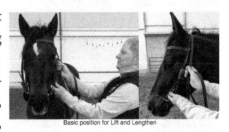

Basic position for Lift and Lengthen

why having a Code, an aid to ask the horse to extend the neck while lightly tightening the reins is an excellent addition to their program. I know you will be so surprised, but...wait for it... I begin by teaching this from the ground.

For an aid to follow a code that keeps the program interconnected and clear, it cannot be one that puts pressure on the tongue with a low or pulling hand or draws the head behind the vertical. So there is a way that avoids both of these pitfalls; **Lift and Lengthen**. We lift the hand and maintain the contact, perhaps even increase it a bit, to ask the horse to take more contact and extend the neck. In short: **Lift** the bit in the mouth and **Lengthen** the neck. This action has several other uses like helping a horse to be willing to take more contact and activating the mouth of a horse who's a bit frozen. As with the other work, this is done from both sides.

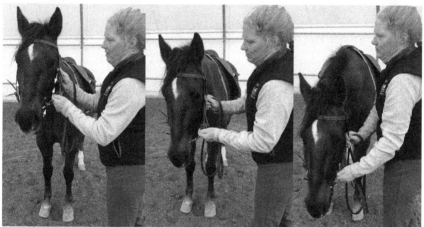

Lift and Lengthen: bring the hands closer together to increase the contact. The horse learns to lengthen the neck.

Working from the horse's left side, the right rein is taken over the poll and into the right hand. The excess rein is taken in a loop in the right hand to prevent the horse from possibly stepping on or through it. When the right rein is drawn down toward the left hand, it will functionally lift the right side of the bit. It will create some poll pressure which can give the horse an idea of the out and downward response we would like him to offer. If the horse overreacts or doesn't tolerate poll pressure there are alternate handholds covered later in this chapter.

The left hand maintains the same handhold as the previous work from the side.

For your Request, lift in the left hand and draw downward with the right hand, essentially bringing the two hands together. It will create an increase of the contact in the bit. The goal is to have the horse extend the neck. When he seeks the answer in that direction, we offer a Reprieve or a lighter contact. With tact and clarity, the horse will understand this Request and we have gained another line of communication to articulate the neck!

Lift and Lengthen: Clearly understood from both sides

The Lift and Lengthen is not a way to force our hand and demand a neck position, but a teaching of a useful Request to help the horse be able to alter neck positions as we would like them to. Lift and Lengthen is most useful when the horse sinks comfortably into the bit stretching and lowering the neck with the nose forward as far as asked. In the end, I like to pause and have the horse show me that we can maintain connection in the lengthened and lower position. This is an access point I want to have under saddle as well so I try to make it as clear as possible from the ground.

If the horse is quite stuck and does not understand the Request, you can gently rock the horse's head from side to side in a slow rhythm to help him get moving in the desired direction. The head should remain vertical as viewed from the front, I just want to gently press into the side of his head to move it a couple of inches to the side away from me and then draw it back those same inches. I'm trying to keep things quiet and calm while loosening his neck a little bit.

If the horse raises his head, maintain the same contact or increase it slightly. This will indicate that his response is not what you are looking for. Again, we are not trying to engage in alligator wrestling, we are trying to teach the horse a new response to the bit. Try your best to stay with the horse keeping very similar contact in the bit. This works also for horses that offer head shaking or moving their head around a great deal as they sort things out. Be patient, stick with them. Especially if the horse is green or has had previous traumatic experiences with the bit. This can take quite a bit of time but the dividends are worth it.

The most simple way to raise the height of the neck is a demi arret in the front hand with the support of the offside rein. The demi arret is for lightening contact that is too heavy, either in a single rein or in both, opening the poll, or raising the height of the neck.

This first alternate application of Lift and Lengthen is to apply the pressure of the off-side rein that would normally go over the poll lower on the neck instead of the poll. This is helpful if the horse has already learned to lower the head by pressure on the poll: not a bad thing at all, but we do

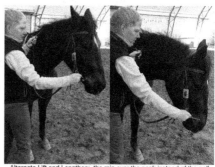

Alternate Lift and Lengthen: the rein over the neck instead of the poll

want the horse to be responding to the bit action, not just the pressure over the poll. This can also be useful for horses that are very poll sensitive or have trauma in the area of the poll or the ears that can cause tension. It can also be a stepping stone toward the sensations from the saddle. The next application is a further step in that particular direction.

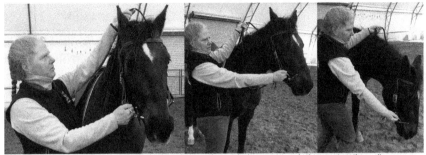

Alternate Lift and Lengthen: the rein over the neck does not touch the crest or the poll

A second alternate application of Lift and Lengthen is the off-side rein over the poll but not in contact with it. Again, with horses that have trauma in the area of the poll, you can use this variation near the poll or further down the neck. You can also use this alternative, especially down the neck if you would like to more closely imitate how the rein effect will feel to the horse from the saddle.

A positive correction can be introduced in the Lift and Lengthen. It involves the horse who over flexes the neck and comes behind the vertical. With this idea in a horse, we must intervene to protect the neck and spinal structures. We begin with the basic Lift and Lengthen aids but we add the forward-moving front hand to take the nose clearly forward. The core problem remains the same; the horse has learned to hide from the bit by flexing behind it. Ultimately he will need to learn the confidence to reach forward/downward into an inviting connection to fully correct the issue. However, this addition of Lift and Lengthen begins to explain to him the forward reach we would like to see in his posture. This

Taking the nose forward in Lift and Lengthen

introduces a physical and mental idea to his reaction to the bit. It's a very difficult situation to fix. The over-flexed position is very stressful for a horse physically and emotionally and it interrupts his vision and center of balance. ***There are no positives in a horse being over flexed.***

Let me repeat this for those in the back: There are no positives in a horse being over flexed regardless of what any trainer may tell you. Science tells us otherwise. And so do the horses. It is much better to avoid over-flexion altogether.

With time and practice, these flexions and actions of the reins will become clear to the horse. A base Code has hopefully been established in the halt. We can now take this Code and further the horse's education as we work in-hand at the walk.

8

In-Hand in the Walk

"Without the encumbrance of your weight, your horse will understand and respond to your demands better and more quickly; you yourself will benefit from your ability to see him; and your hand, closer to his mouth, will act more clearly and effectively. So begin your work on foot." ~Jean Froissard

Working in-hand in the walk brings us one step closer to what the horse will likely feel from the reins under the saddle. Again, from the ground, we can see our horse's mouth, the bit, the actions of our hands, and our horse's reaction.

Working in the walk is an amazing way to educate the driving horse. With ponies and minis, it can be the best way to clarify rein aids, flexion, and balance as they are sometimes too small to ride. In-hand walk work is an exceptional tool for horses rehabilitating from an injury. This work is practically the only way to rebuild the confidence of a horse who has experienced trauma in his mouth, especially from the saddle. The work is mentally stimulating while non-concussive physically.

Mary and her driving pony, Chili

A session of in-hand work, including the walk, is a lovely companion for a lunge day. It gives the horse's body a bit of a break while tuning the most refined part of the entire instrument that we refer to as our horse.

Nearly every concept that we would like the horse to understand from the saddle can be taught and practiced from the ground. We start with informing the responses in the mouth in simple transitions, changing the balance, and changing the gaits. We can then move on to lateral movements; shoulder-in, renvers, travers, half pass. The advanced work can include jambette, Spanish walk, piaffe, passage, levade, and more. If your goals aren't quite so lofty, the basic flexions in motion are of exceptional benefit for any horse.

A big part of the challenge of the walking work in-hand is *the walking*. The positive side of this is the opportunity to better learn how to use our hands independently from our bodies while we are in motion. The negative side is that it's a lot to think about. Now instead of being able to

Jambette Left Leg

focus directly on the mouth, the horse's reaction, our requests, the response the horse offers, the corrections we offer...we do all of this and then add in walking for both ourselves and the horse. Our balance will be changing. The horse's balance will be changing. It may seem simple but I'm giving you a heads up: this work is challenging but the positive results are worth it! I hope you can see the wisdom of developing the work in-hand in the halt to clarity before moving on to the walk.

The Code for the basic in-hand work includes **hand position, body position, whip position/aids, rein aids**, and **voice aids**. If we keep to the Code in all of our aids, we can expect to have a reliable response from our horse with time, consistency, and repetition. Remember, the way we use all of the aids remains the same: Request, Reprieve, Resist, Release.

Hand Position

The basic hand positions for the walk work are the same as the position we were using in the flexions from the side: front hand in the ring of the bit and rear hand holding the offside rein over the neck on the shoulder. This is a workable and utilitarian hand position. Even in the walk, we want to stay equidistant between the hands as much as possible. There are variations to this basic position to meet different needs and preferences but this position should get you started.

The back of the rear hand fingers is often resting on the shoulder. This helps you to stay in sync with your horse. You'll be able to match his changes of balance and walk tempo without having to look at him. This gives you more freedom to check on other things you might be working on.

There are times, which I will try to mention or point out, where bringing the rear hand off the shoulder is helpful. It will also come into use that the rear hand presses into the shoulder to request that the shoulder weight change away from us.

Body Position

Regardless of which side you work from (yes, we will work from both sides) we indicate the walk by turning to face forward. For the halt, we return to the position facing the horse. For rein back, we will turn to face the rear of the horse. As the horse becomes more familiar with the work, the change in body position will be a key indicator of forward and backward so you will need the whip and bit aids progressively more subtlely.

Body position for Reinback   Body position for Halt   Body position for Walk

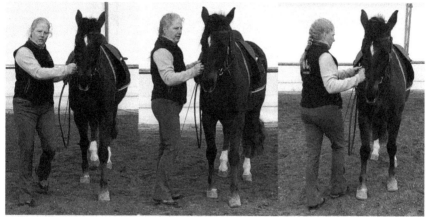

Working position from the right side in walk, halt, and reinback

Working positions: Reinback-Face the rear   Halt-Face the horse   Walk-face forward

The Whip

The whip will indicate movement forward and the yielding of the haunches, just as the legs do under saddle. As we try our best to have a Code that the horse can depend on, we want to keep a Code for the whip position.

Neutral Go Forward Yield the Haunches

We hold the whip in the rear hand that is holding the offside rein. When the whip is straight up and down, this is the neutral position. For the horse to move forward, we will rotate our wrist so the whip can touch the torso of the horse to tap until the horse moves forward and return to the neutral position. When we advance to moving the haunches, the whip will be held in a horizontal position to indicate to the haunches to shift away from us.

A temptation to avoid is trying to talk the horse into going forward by pulling on the bit. This is not the bit's job and it creates ill-defined movement in the mouth. Be clear and repeatedly tap on the torso with the whip and send the horse forward in unison with your movement, perhaps even a little before you at first. In time, the other aids should suffice and you will use the whip aids less as a basic aid and more as a reminder.

Rein Aids

The rein aids will be similar to but simpler than those used under saddle. This is due to the limitation of being on one side of the horse at a time. Nevertheless, the rein aids will create much better education in contact, raising and lowering the neck, flexions, and relaxation. The front hand will be in the bit ring so we have the clearest feeling of what is happening in the mouth. A temptation with the front hand will be to pull back and push forward but the majority of the aids in the front hand will be following and lifting. That's the reason we keep the thumb over the cheekpiece is to remind us not to pull back or down if we can avoid it.

The rear hand, working from its place on the shoulder, will have the action of drawing straight down for slowing or runback, supporting demi arret, and requesting flexion away from us when the time comes. Some alternatives are the same as the previous chapter on working in-hand from the side:

Basic action of the hands for rein back and demi arret

using the offside rein with no contact on the crest of the neck, and working over the poll, especially for relaxation of the jaw, and Lift and Lengthen.

Voice Aids

In the past, I've not been a big fan of voice aids but as I began more involvement in carriage driving I saw a very supportive role they can play both in-hand and under saddle. The crucial role of voice aids in driving is obvious but they are helpful in other work as well. The in-hand work in the walk can be another place the driving horse becomes more and more familiar with the voice commands you will use when driving. I keep my voice commands simple and consistent. I believe that the tone and pitch of the voice command are more influential than the actual words but I keep the words and sounds the same too. Whatever you choose, keep to your Code so your horse knows exactly what is expected of him.

My Code for my horses, as far as sounds go, is clucking with the tongue twice means walk to trot. A smooching sound means canter. Repeated clucking means to continue to add energy.

My voice commands include, " Walk." "Walk on." "Trot." "Easy." "Canter." "Woah." "Back." "Come." If I'm going down a gait, I will say, "Ea-sy walk," all in a descending set of pitches. If I want to go faster or add energy I'll say, "Walk on," in an ascending pitch or the same pitch. "Come," is a voice command for me that means, "I want more of that." "Trot," and "Canter," are self-explanatory. As a musician, I can't help notating things like pitch and tone in my mind. I think of voice aids as supportive to the physical aids like reins, legs, seat, whip, etc.

Let's Get Walking

Working with a timid young or inexperienced horse, I might start the walk work in a halter as I may have done with the flexions. The horse may not be used to me walking with them in this position. While we are at it, we can make sure the horse understands the body position, voice aids, and whip aids in the walk while they are in a halter or cavesson. You may have covered these bases with groundwork and lunging but in case you haven't, it would be a good idea to make sure the horse is clear on all of these aids in motion. Particularly fearful or tense horses may need this confidence-building step.

With the bit, we are trying to build a sophisticated communication system. Tension and fear will only muddy the waters. We don't want the horse to overreact while we are holding on to the bit and have it tumble around in his mouth. That would only add a negative association.

The basics I want to cover are: walk, halt, rein back, Lift and Lengthen, and Shift the Shoulders. You can be thorough and teach all of these in a halter before working with the bit, especially if you feel it would benefit your horse. Once the horse understands how to walk with you in the position of the in-hand work on both sides, you can feel pretty confident that we will be able to focus on the education of the bit while moving.

I usually start the walk work from the left side as the horse is usually more familiar with me there. (Of course, I will repeat all the work on the right side as well.) Begin the walk work on the wall for the support and straightness it can offer on your offside.

I stand in the halt position, turn to face forward, cluck or ask "Walk," and touch the horse's torso with the whip if needed. When the horse begins to walk, my first job is to follow the mouth in my left hand as the head and neck undulate rhythmically with the stride of each front leg. If I don't follow well, the horse will bump into the bit. At best he could become annoyed or perceive the random movements of the bit in his mouth as "white noise." At worst, tension could spread from his mouth through the neck and back causing dysfunctional movement in the walk. Learning the dance moves of the neck and head and learning to join in with the hand is one of the benefits of the work in the walk.

If the horse is walking too slow, a cluck and a tap with the whip should take care of it. If needed, you can use a repeated tapping with the whip to say, "I'm staying here to bother you until you make a change." When he increases his energy forward, stop the tapping. He should get the idea. Do not try to pull him forward with the bit. It is his job to learn to match your tempo.

If the horse is walking much too briskly, you have two options: let him walk a circle around you while you stay in a neutral position on a very small circle. You can even rotate on the spot and let him walk. The deviation and balance it takes to walk a very small circle could work to relax him. You can even add a flexion of the neck to the inside to stretch the outside of the neck. The second option is a demi arret (or repeated demi arrets) to ask him to slow down.

If I am following well and the horse remains relaxed, carrying his head and neck in a straight, medium position, I can then check his tracking. Are his hind feet stepping along the same line as his front feet? Is the horse crooked and the hind feet tracking inside or outside? This is part of noting the horse's tendencies and asymmetries. The corrections will come later.

Once the horse is walking fairly straight, you are coordinated in the hands, you can work on balanced halts. A balanced halt is one that isn't in a "falling forward" balance, where the horse is synchronized with you and your aids, where the head and neck stay in the requested position.

To halt, slow your walking steps and begin to turn toward him while lifting in the front hand and drawing down in the rear hand. At the same time give him the verbal cue, "Woah." If he doesn't respond well and keeps moving forward, you can use repeated demi arrets in both hands while raising his neck a little bit to help shift some weight to the rear. If even this doesn't help and he's still determined to move forward, you may need to return to a cavesson or a halter to clarify the aids.

Once your horse is immobile, give him a break, drop the reins and scratch him. We would like to keep the halt a "break room" that he wants to be in. It's part of a reward system and can also be used as part of positive reinforcement. Of course, you don't have to do this on every halt, but keep it in mind to create not only a physical halt but an emotional one as well. Once the horse understands walk to halt without confusion or inconsistencies, you can use transitions between walk and halt to fine-tune the horse's attention to you and his balance.

For reinback, use the same upward action in the front hand and the downward draw of the rear hand until the horse shifts his weight backward. Support with the voice command, "back." Release and begin the process again until the steps become steadier and the weight shift is easier. It's better to ask lightly 10 times for 10 steps than to ask rudely once for a resentful response. We do not want to create backward traction on the mouth but an indication of what we have asked for.

It may seem simple, but a prompt walk depart, straight and in unity, a balanced halt, and an organized weight shift for rein back is not so easy. Once you can perform these transitions on the wall for straightness support, we can begin to explore work off the wall.

Shift the Shoulders

We have already discussed that 2/3 of the horse's weight is on the forehand. It would seem that the best use of time and focus would be to create mobility in those shoulders. That mobility would affect the bulk of the weight centered in the horse.

Shift the Shoulders: Shoulders right with left flexion

I have heard many times the phrase "dropping the shoulder." I believe that language is important and the accuracy of the language will make concepts clearer. Clearer concepts lead to more effective solutions. instead of thinking about a horse dropping a shoulder or a rider lifting a shoulder perhaps a more accurate way of thinking about it is to address how much of the balance is too far over a shoulder. There is too much weight over one shoulder and not enough over the other. (There are more complexities in weight distribution and asymmetry that we can discuss later, but this is a good beginning).

Having a Code to change the weight from one shoulder to the other is a straightforward way to alter and begin to correct the lateral balance. That's where we can start teaching the horse to Shift the Shoulders: take the weight from one shoulder to the other as requested. If the shoulders are accessible and mobile, it's less likely the horse will park so much weight over one or the other.

We begin this exercise in the walk off the wall with some room on the off-side of our horse. In the walk, begin to ask the horse to step away from you in rhythm with his stride. You are walking an arc or a circle away from you by simply moving the shoulders. You can do this with a flexion toward you, a straight neck, or a flexion away. Your hand on the shoulder with support from your hand at the bit creates a similar effect to a neck rein.

At first, the coordination of walking and shifting the shoulders could prove difficult for your horse. If you need to, go back to working in a halter and teach him to move his shoulders away from pressure on the shoulder with support from the front hand lightly holding the noseband of the halter. When he moves away with understanding and fluidity on both sides, you can return to the work with the bit.

If the horse continues to struggle, you can raise the neck with your front hand on the bit and add a bit of flexion toward you. Sometimes this can help.

Shift the Shoulders: shoulders left with straight neck

Immobile shoulders are a formidable obstacle to both longitudinal and lateral balance and habitually weighting one shoulder more than the other is part of the horse's natural asymmetry.

Flechit Droit

Flechit Droit (flexion on a straight line) is a stretching and balancing exercise that can be used to explain to a horse that the flexion and the direction do not have to be one and the same. Flechit droit develops changes in balance and flexibility. We would like to be able to control flexion and di-

The flexion can free the movement of the outside shoulder

rection and ask for them separately depending on the need. Back on the wall, ask for the walk with the horse tracking straight. Using a lifting and drawing toward you in the front hand, ask for the amount of flexion the horse can offer comfortably in the walk. Use your rear hand to put enough pressure on the shoulder to request the shoulders stay in alignment with the haunches. The Shift the Shoulders should have helped this to become clear enough to do this exercise fairly easily.

Flechit droit right   Flechit droit left

When flechit droit is well understood, the horse can organize his balance through his forehand with the neck straight as well as in a flexion. This gives us the option of neck placement laterally without it being automatically linked to the direction the horse travels. This is very nice to have especially on voltes and arced lines. With this understanding, we can change the amount of neck flexion as needed without interrupting the balance. Flechit droit is also very helpful in addressing asymmetry in the horse's body.

Adjusting Head/Neck Height and Posture

Lift and Lengthen

Alternative Lift and Lengthen with the offside rein over the mid-neck instead of over the poll

The same aids for the same goals for Lift and Lengthen can be done in the walk as was used in the halt. For Lift and Lengthen at the walk you will need to put your whip down. Your rear hand will either be at your horse's mid-neck or holding the rein that is over the poll. Because of this, you and your horse will need to have a clear halt to walk transitions without using a whip. You have a couple of choices of how to go about Lift and Lengthen in the walk: In the halt, arrange your reins as you would for Lift and Lengthen in the halt. Ask the horse to "walk," perhaps offer a cluck. Once walking, begin to apply the Lift and Lengthen aids. If the horse begins to offer either the improved mobility of the mouth or the lengthening of the neck, soften the aids and stop to rest and give him a scratch.

Lift and Lengthen in the rein position over the poll at the walk

The second choice is to begin as you would normally and move the rein to the Lift and Lengthen position while you are in the walk. Either can be used based on what is going to be more efficient and effective for the situation. If your horse gets really confused while trying this at the walk, go ahead and halt to repeat what he knows well. Then see which approach will help him understand the aids while walking. With time and patience, this will begin to become clear. Remember, it isn't a wrestling match. We are teaching and rewarding.

Alternative Lift and Lengthen holding both reins

A similar alternative can be used with the offside rein brought over the mid-neck for Lift and Lengthen. It is helpful for creating an effect closer to what the horse will experience under saddle or when being driven. You can further this idea by holding both reins with your rear arm over the horse's neck holding the offside rein and your front hand holding the rein instead of the bit. I use this if the horse needs another "half-step" in their education. This is a must for the horses I'm preparing as carriage driving horses.

The Overflexed Horse

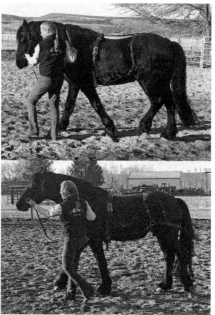

We began to address the overflexion of the neck at the halt. You can continue to correct this unhealthful posture in the walk work. A horse who is over flexed or hiding behind the bit is avoiding communication and connection. The simplest correction is to take your front hand forward to offer a horse a different physical position in the walk just as we did in the halt. The root problem is a lack of confidence in taking a clear

Emphasizing "nose forward" while we work in-hand at the walk contact in the bit. This is a tricky and time-consuming issue to fix. *It is much better to avoid over-flexion altogether.*

The goal is a synchronous dance. The horse has a much better opportunity to stay in agreement with you when he can see you more than when you are on his back. He now can Take advantage of this! Take your time. Enjoy the process. Give your horse the benefit of learning within his strengths and in the walk where you both have time to make changes and corrections. Trot, lateral movements, and collected movements are further on with this program. There is always more you can learn. If you can master these basics, not only will the more advanced work come more easily, you will have gained mutual understanding with your horse with the bit and the rein aids.

9

Under Saddle

> *"In the case of equilibrium it is the horse's acceptance of the rider's hand actions, in a spirit of confidence and submission, that is most important. Without it, the horse's proper use of its head and neck, an absolutely essential balancing pole in its equilibration, is bound to be more or less detrimentally affected." ~Jean Saint-Fort Paillard (1913-1990)*

In my early years on Buck, the head, the neck, and the reins attached were simply for steering and stopping. I had some idea about "headset," the way the horse was "supposed" to carry his head and neck but I didn't know why they should do that besides the judges at the horse shows liked it.

I was vaguely aware of acting in a fair manner with my hand

Buck and I in the early 1980's

and the reins, but truth be told, I was young and could be impatient. The examples around me weren't helpful either as horses' heads were tied down or bits used to purposefully cause pain so the horse would stay in the "proper position" on a loose rein. There wasn't much, if any, real awareness of the mouth, the education, the sensitivity, and the interconnectedness of the mouth and jaw to the rest of the horse. I saw a lot of suffering because of it. Sadly, it took decades for me to find access to what has been the solution for me and the students I strive to educate, both horse and human.

We've discussed the head and neck as a significant element of lateral and longitudinal balance. We have begun to educate our horses on the ground to the sensations of the bit, how to stay relaxed and softly handle the bit. We have pushed ourselves to educate our own hands and the actions they can take to communicate to the horse through contact with the bit or through the reins. Now we take this education and teach the horse the code from the saddle.

I've come across a common way of describing the lateral effects of the reins in the French equitation literature. Although the 5 or 6 rein effects they discuss can work very well in both theory and practice, I think it's needlessly complicated. If we begin with clear, fairly simple, and utilitarian roles for the rein positions and the expectations from these positions, slight modifications and greater nuance can come later.

Now we need to remember the ways in which the aids can be used in general: **Request, Reprieve, Resist, Release**. These uses continue into the rein effects. With the differing positions of the reins coupled with the ways in which we use our hands, you have, if my math is correct, 27 combinations available to you times the above four uses of the hand! If you become adept at using this code, your horse will be able to more fully participate because he understands clearly.

Lateral Rein Aids

There are three basic positions I use for the lateral rein aids under saddle. Keep clearly in mind that The Code is only as good as it is taught to the horse. There's no magic sauce aid in the reins that horses are born knowing. Horses can learn through repetition and They can be used individually on

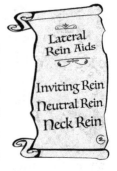

Lateral
Rein Aids

Inviting Rein
Neutral Rein
Neck Rein

one side or concurrently with the same or another rein effect on the other side. They can also be used to varying degrees from a slight suggestion to really trying to spell things out for the horse. The three rein positions I like to talk about are the **Inviting Rein**, the **Neck Rein**, and the **Neutral Rein**.

The Inviting Rein

Is often referred to as an opening or direct rein. To offer an Inviting Rein, leave the elbow low and swivel the acting hand and arm out to the side as if you are opening a door. Try to keep the arm bent and relaxed with the thumb more or less up. The inviting rein speaks to the direction of the shoulders on the side it is applied.

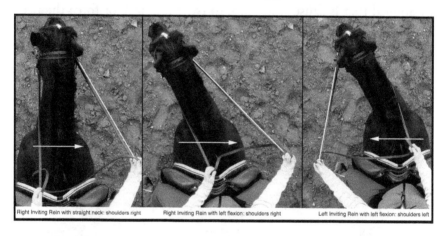

Right Inviting Rein with straight neck: shoulders right   Right Inviting Rein with left flexion: shoulders right   Left Inviting Rein with left flexion: shoulders left

The effect of "direct rein" is a bit misleading because that description matches if I'm using an Inviting Rein on the side of the neck flexion. The horse directly follows it with his head. However, if I use an Inviting Rein on the opposite side of the flexion, I'm inviting the shoulders to shift (even slightly) to the direction opposite the flexion. (In my example in the photos I am using a right Inviting Rein with a left Neck Rein so I very much am asking for the shoulders to go right.) I also like to use the word "Inviting" because it is closer to my intent. I don't want to demand the horse to follow a direct rein, I want to invite the horse to join me with the weight of his shoulders. This position and its effects can be used with a straight neck, on the inside or the outside of the flexion. The shoulders follow the Inviting Rein regardless of the flexion of the neck. This provides many applications of this rein position for prescribing separately the neck flexion and the direction of travel of the shoulders as well as the rest of the body.

The Neck Rein

The Neck Rein is as it is named. Pretty simple. The contact of the Neck Rein, regardless of the flexion, indicates a change of weight to the opposite shoulder. To apply the neck rein, the hand moves up and toward the opposite shoulder (to make sure we have the lifting effect in the mouth of the bit). It is not the intent of the neck rein to be so heavily applied that it causes the horse to twist the neck or force the neck to change the flexion. As the horse understands more clearly, the rein touching the neck will indicate to the horse to change the weighting of the shoulders.

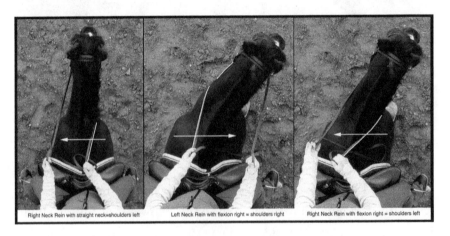

Right Neck Rein with straight neck=shoulders left   Left Neck Rein with flexion right = shoulders right   Right Neck Rein with flexion right = shoulders left

It is widely believed that the western disciplines invented this rein position and its effects. From Medieval Knights to WWII cavalry, mounted battle required the ability to use one hand to guide their horse and the other to wield a weapon. The Neck Rein can be used for far more than turning to face the foe in battle.

Its effects can yield amazing abilities to shift the weight correctly for balance and straightness of the horse. In time, the mere contact of the rein can indicate the aid. The Neck Rein can be used with a straight neck and on the inside or the outside of the flexion.

The movement to apply a Neck Rein is a lifting in the direction of the shoulder opposite the hand applying the aid. The elbows stay heavy, the wrist fairly straight. Think of a suggestion of "embracing" the part of the neck you would like to apply the Neck Rein to.   An embrace helps prevent us from simply dragging the rein across the shoulders and shoving the horse around. The embrace is a comforting and guiding feeling like helping a child make his way. With the embrace, I say with my intent, "Come with me." If the horse hears me and tries to shift the weight, I greatly soften the Neck Rein and ask again. Soon the horse will appreciate such a warm and clear guidance and the shoulders will become supple and mobile.

The Neutral Rein

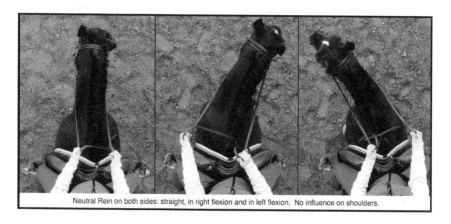

Neutral Rein on both sides: straight, in right flexion and in left flexion. No influence on shoulders.

The central role of a neutral rein is to influence the mouth or the flexion of the neck without direct contact or influence of the neck or shoulders. Applying the Neutral Rein is a lifting action of the hand in such a way that the rein doesn't significantly touch the neck. The direction of the hand when applying the neutral rein varies with the flexion of the neck. The Neutral Rein is most often used to communicate the amount of flexion in the neck without changing the lateral balance over the shoulders or changing direction. Think of it as if you want the rein opposite of the Neutral Rein to be more influential and the Neutral Rein to stay out of the way while maintaining the desired contact or flexion. Another use is "gathering" the shoulders between the reins or neutralizing some of the effects of an Inviting Rein or Neck Rein.

For instance, a left Neck Rein with a Right Inviting rein will indicate to the horse "I really want you to go to the right." A left Neck Rein with a Right Neutral rein softens that request a bit. It can be used to help stabilize the height of the head, help the horse have more confidence in the contact with one rein at a time, ask for more contact, and ask for a release of the jaw. The Neutral Rein can be used, like the others, with a straight neck, inside or outside of the flexion.

"The rider provides himself with the means of placing the horse's head and neck in the position that he wishes and of inducing the horse to assume this position without any muscular contractions other than those required to assume it." From this point on, always naturally, a change of position is necessarily accompanied by a related change of equilibrium....and the desired movement is produced as if it were performed by the horse of its own volition."
~Jean Saint-Fort Paillard

With the understanding of the individual effects of the three rein aid positions on each side of the neck, we can discuss the combination effects. Knowing the combinations and the goals of clarity we seek to impart, we can teach this code. By following it, we have reliable means of influencing two-thirds of the horse's weight which is located shoulders forward.

Rein Combinations~Straight Neck

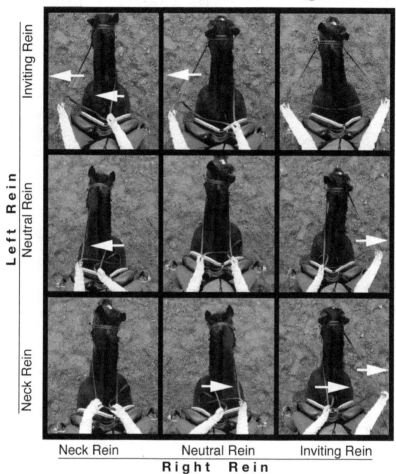

The main reason I prefer to ride with the hands further apart than some is that I don't want to be applying a Neck Rein effect on both sides of the neck at one time (picture in lower left of Rein Combinations in Straight neck, next page). I want the contact of the rein against the neck to indicate the movement of the shoulders in the opposite direction.

In the upper-right photograph of the same grid, I'm using an Inviting Rein in both hands. A benefit of this rein effect is a more oblique angle toward the bit that many horses are more willing to receive. Horses that struggle to offer an authentic contac and those that are shy about input from the bit can benefit from this position. The Inviting Rein in both hands can serve as a funnel for a wiggly young horse as well, showing them a bigger target to hit to find their way in my contact.

Rein Combinations~Left Flexion

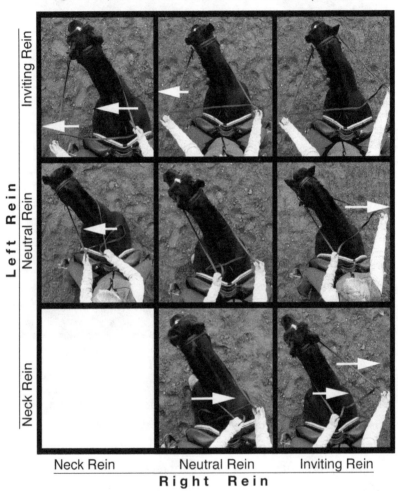

The arrows are pretty self-explanatory. For instance, a combination of an Inviting Rein in one hand and a Neck Rein in the other, regardless of flexion, is a very clear message for the horse to move the shoulders. Just how much is up to the discretion and sensibilities of the rider.

Rein Combinations~Right Flexion

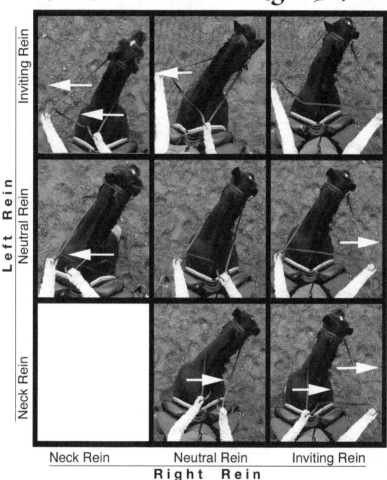

Longitudinal Rein Aids

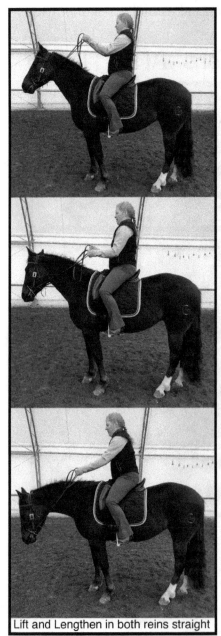

Lift and Lengthen in both reins straight

Longitudinal
Rein Aids

Demi arret
Lift & Lengthen

Now that we have looked at the lateral rein aids and their effects, we now turn our attention to the longitudinal rein aids to change the height and posture of the neck. We saw clearly in the chapter on the neck that the position of the neck affects the balance of the horse to a large degree. Having aids in place to communicate those positions will prove very helpful. Aren't we glad we have already introduced and codified these aids from the ground?

Welcome back to Lift and Lengthen. Lift and Lengthen from the saddle has the same purpose and is looking for the same results as when we used it from the ground. It is the guidance for the horse to take more contact in the rein. This effect is especially useful in the cases of a horse reversing the neck or being above the hand.

(A horse can't technically be above the hand if the hand is above the mouth!)

Lift and Lengthen can activate the mouth or extend the neck based on how the aids are applied. Lift and Lengthen can be requested straight, in a flexion either way or with one rein at a time. Lift and Lengthen can be done with the hands the same width apart or widening the hands to offer a milder effect. Regardless of the indication for use, the *bottom line for Lift and Lengthen is to improve the contact.*

You may have been told to fix your hands in a low position if a horse's head is "too high." There is a significant problem with this hand position: it is putting direct pressure on the tongue and bars. If the horse does bring his head down, it will be reactionary, not because of understanding. The contact with the bit will be something to avoid and you will likely then have a horse unwilling to maintain any meaningful contact. He will probably hide behind the bit in overflexion as well.

First, we explain to the horse that the contact will remain, albeit painlessly, regardless of his neck position. Then we listen very carefully

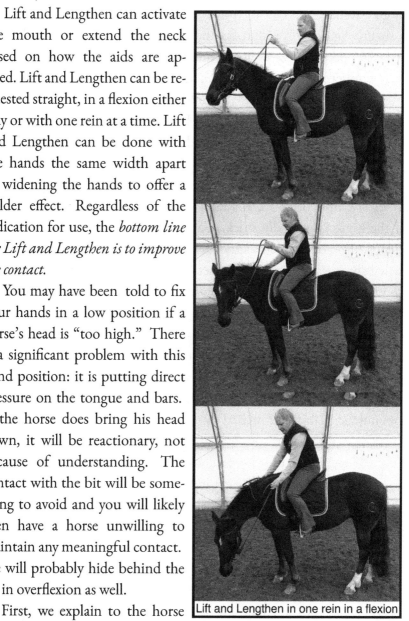

Lift and Lengthen in one rein in a flexion

for the horse to nudge the contact forward and downward. It's as if he's asking, "If the contact is staying, can I find a more comfortable position?" "What a great idea!" you say as you follow him while maintaining a slightly lighter contact. It may be a simple idea but that doesn't make it easy to do. There are a lot of questions to answer in every situation. "How much contact?" "How much do you lighten the contact when they try to reach into it?" "Should you increase the contact if the horse doesn't seem to respond?" "How much should you increase the contact?" The answers, unfortunately, fall under *it depends*. No really! It does! This is an explanation from you of what you would like for the horse to do and I'm not there to listen to his reply; you are.

A few tips to try are 1. adding a flexion to the Lift and Lengthen if the horse is mentally stuck in a high position. 2. Try the Lift and Lengthen in one rein at a time. Really focus and feel for that moment when the horse has the idea of settling into the contact and offer him something lighter. Lift and Lengthen may be easier for him to understand in the walk or even in the trot.

Activating the mouth is another use for Lift and Lengthen. You can separate your hands and see if that is enough for the horse to mobilize the jaw. If not, a flexion using the lifting inside rein and observing the mouth to see if it becomes mobile. The mobility of the mouth will also be more available and relaxed as your hand learns to follow even the small movements of the tongue and jaw. It's much more inviting to the horse when he feels that you can hear him and join in.

The last and most subtle use in Lift and Lengthen is the request for increased contact. I missed this detail in some horses for a long time. In this application, I mainly use the widened hands, like if I was offering two Inviting Reins at the same time. I keep the tension in a lateral direction; the hands continuing to widen until the horse increases the contact and settles into it. As the horse takes a more significant connection with the bit, I allow my hands and arms to come back together. With my thumbs pointed up and out, I am not in a position to pull backward and risk the horse coming behind the bit. The horse can tell the difference: widening the hands increases the contact on the corners of the lips without direct pressure on the tongue.

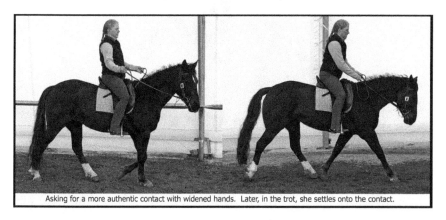

Asking for a more authentic contact with widened hands. Later, in the trot, she settles onto the contact.

When the horse is floating even a little above the contact, isn't actually contact. It's a shadow or a wisp. I've noticed that horses can be consistent in their posture but the contact they are offering is not authentic. The horse isn't fully there ON the hand in full trust of the connection. This has led to inconsistencies in the neck height and head posture which leads to inconsistencies in the balance. I felt as if I were chasing the contact and hoping for the best instead of spending the effort, observation, and time to develop a genuine connection.

This kind of connection is not pulling but also not floating. Using authentic contact, the horse begins to develop a positive integrated function throughout the body. It sounds like hogwash, but it's the reality when the muscle, fascia, emotion, and mind all cooperate in harmony. Horses can function without this kind of contact, but if I'm asking for so much more than basic level function, I feel I must raise my input to facilitate extraordinarily tuned responses in the horse. It's a joy for me and it's beneficial for the horse.

Clear contact out and down can aid the lifting of the thoracic sling and healtheir function of the lumbar spine

Codified, effective, and efficient rein aids might seem to be too complex to be worth the time and repetition. When the horse understands what is being asked of him, it is because someone taught it to him. With that understanding comes confidence and relaxation and cooperation. Cooperation becomes an easy choice when there is no reason to be confused or frustrated.

> *"Above all, lightness finds its expression in the submission of the jaw which is the first area (joint) receiving the effect of the hand, thus its submission becomes evident when it responds with elasticity and springiness to the action that solicits its play."*
> ~*General Alexis L'Hotte (1825-1904)*

The "Spring System" of Contact

I would like to briefly explain the concept of maintaining the springs that make the kind of connection we are looking for possible. Each part plays a role in the line of communication staying open and vibrant. Each part also plays its specific role in the healthful qualities of contact: relaxation, communication, balance, alignment, and proper muscular function.

The springs in the horse most active in the contact are the mouth, the jaw, and the poll. We activate them in that order as poll flexion without the first two springs, is simply an evasion or learned response. Poll flexion alone doesn't engage the full system.

In the rider, the spring system contains the fingers, the wrist, the elbows, and the shoulders. We looked at this a little bit in Chapter 2. The greatest complexity of communication comes through the fingers and the least from the shoulders. This is why we put so much emphasis on educating the rider's hands.

The main springs in the system of contact

The most direct connection is from the hand to the mouth. The lips and the tongue receive the message. In the best scenario, the rest of the system engages. A request causes the initiation of a cycle of action and counteraction creating buoyant, elasticized, positive responses back and forth between horse and rider. It is a wondrous feeling when it "clicks" into action.

If any of the individual springs of the system is stuck, the whole system functions poorly, if at all. This means if the mouth is tense, poll flexion is meaningless. If the elbow is locked, the jaw mobility becomes blocked.

There exists the study of spring systems and networks in engineering and physics. Stated without mathematical formulae, if one spring in a network ceases to function, all of the springs in the network are affected. This spring system is no different.

It is incredibly difficult to put perception and feeling into words. Many, many have tried. I hope that these photos and descriptions can help you find your way to a more meaningful connection between you and your horse through contact.

10

The Gaits and Connection

The conundrum at hand (pun intended) is the endless ways the two beings can move both with and against one another. Even in the three basic gaits, the interaction between these moving entities shows inevitable complications. Each horse's gaits are individual to their conformation, education, fitness, and balance. One horse's trot may be easy to sit while another could jar the fillings out of your teeth. It's the same with the canter. You could enjoy a nice "rocking horse canter" with one horse while you can hardly stay settled in the saddle cantering a different horse. Put simply, riding isn't easy, and trying to develop a cooperative relationship with your horse through the mouth is complex. Have I said it enough times for you to get the idea? I don't want to discourage you! I want you to be encouraged knowing that the goals you have are attainable with quality guidance, understanding the work ahead of you, and a lot of focused practice.

I have included both photos and drawings to illustrate the interaction between me and the two horses I am riding. The photos are of Kali, a 6-year-old Hackney Horse cross mare. The drawings are from a video taken of Pickle, a Quarter Horse gelding. Every horse's gaits have unique qualities but the basics remain the same: walk, trot, and canter.

The Walk

In the walk: as each front leg swings forward, the neck stretchs forward as well.

At the walk, a four-beat gait with no moments of suspension, the horse needs to undulate the neck both up and down as well as forward and back during the cycle of strides. If the connection doesn't follow this motion or restricts it, the back of the horse doesn't function correctly. During the stride to maintain the same amount of ounces in each hand, the hands must follow the mouth forward and downward with the opening and closing of the elbows and articulation of the shoulders. The wrists and fingers can add some shock absorption to maintain a welcome connection for the horse.

The Quarter Horse gelding naturally has more movement in his neck than the Hackney mare. It's up to me to find his range of motion in his neck along with the rhythm in which he uses it. Then I allow all the joints from my shoulders to my fingers to soften and match it.

Sometimes I will say to my students, "My hands belong to the horse," when I want them to think more about allowing the horse to "lead the dance." Let the horse take your hand and guide you to the place he needs you to be for him. Later, after you can easily maintain the connection, you have gained the skill to lead the dance. To make small changes to the steps and the postures. And your Requests will be clear and welcome by the horse.

In the French tradition, the walk is referred to as "The Queen of Gaits" because of the multiple benefits gained by its use. The walk is where the rider can most easily teach the horse the contact because it is slow and rhythmic and the horse is not emotionally stirred by speed. It is referred to as "faire la bouche," or "familiarizing the horse to the bit." The same is true of the walk for the benefit of teaching the horse rein aids of all kinds and lateral movements when the time comes.

The 18th-century ecuyer François de Lubersac, from the acclaimed School of Versailles, was credited with educating his horses entirely at the walk. When the time came for trot and canter work, the horses were found to be perfectly schooled for and in all gaits. At one time the FEI Dressage Rules stated that "it is at the pace of walk that the imperfections of dressage are most evident." The walk is slow enough to teach, to feel, to think, and to come to understanding. Don't make the mistake of overlooking the benefits.

LINDA KAYE HOLLINGSWORTH-JONES

The Trot

This may be an appropriate head and neck posture for a young or green horse learning about contact

In the trot, the horse has diagonal legs in flight and weight-bearing in pairs that alternate to spring the horse forward over the ground. This brings about the characteristic bounce and one-two-one-two rhythm. You can think of the motion through the trunk as more like a "fish" movement; swinging back and forth with the belly and torso. The horse's neck doesn't tend to move a great deal as it does in the walk and canter, but WE do! Sitting and posting, our position is changing with each stride. if we do not compensate to keep the same connection with the horse, we will unwittingly bump the mouth regularly or have continuous interruption of the communication. Either of these situations will disturb the balance and organization of the horse.

In the sitting trot (drawings, next page) the elbows must open and close slightly to keep the level of the hands the same as the level of the mouth to keep the bit from bouncing in the horse's mouth. I want to mention that sitting the trot is not some kind of rite of passage. We only have so many hours of sitting trot in our own bodies and the horses only have so much tolerance for my imperfect sitting trot! Nobody is a lesser rider for posting the trot to ease their own back as well as that of their horse.

In the posting trot (below) this becomes even more exaggerated as I rise higher in the posting motion than I was in the sitting trot.

A more complex conversation: maintaining connection while requesting a specific position in the neck

As the horse's education commences, requesting a specific neck position adds to the complexities of riding each gait.

The communication becomes more and more layered as the basic contact is further modified by perhaps a flexion of the neck, horizontal position changes (that we talked about in Chapter 9), and the later addition of poll flexion (to be discussed in future works). The relationship of the hand to the mouth is what is key, not the relationship of the hand to me or how my seat and the rest of my body are moving to follow the motions of the trunk of the horse.

The Canter

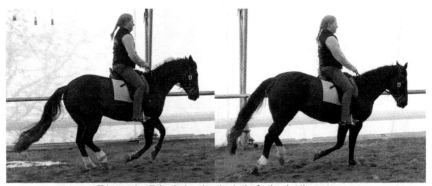

This mare is still developing elevation in the forehand at the canter

The definition of the canter is a three-beat gait with a moment of suspension. The first beat is the outside hind leg, followed by the lateral pair then the inside front. The horse's body works in more of a "dolphin" movement through the trunk (sometimes called "bascule" when referring to the more significant expression of this movement over jumps). The canter feels like a rocking motion when riding and can be comfortable to ride or quite a challenge depending on the horse.

In the photos and the drawings, I tried to find moments at both extremes of the stride cycle where the mouth is closest to me and farthest away. This can be the point where the horse is most elevated front to back and then the opposite where the front end is down and the quarters are up recycling for the next stride.

Not only do I have to build up my strength and balance to be able to sit upright in the canter throughout the canter stride, but my hands must follow the up/down and forward/back motion of the neck/mouth as I am doing the opposite! When his weight and stride are the most forward, I am sitting the farthest back and vice versa. I have found the canter the most challenging to help my students find balance both in their seat and in their connection.

Staying connected with two horses who have grown into forehand elevation in canter

The canter is a gait that shows a great deal of change from one horse to another and in a horse as his education grows. A disorganized canter is very difficult to ride at all without even trying to keep the contact!

To further complicate things, the canter tends to magnify the horse's emotions: fear, anxiety, play, frustration, tension all come closer to the surface when working in the canter. All of these elements make the canter more complex than walk or trot.

As a trainer, it's my job to ride the canter the horse has at the time. It could bring any selection of things for me to handle and also try to continue the horse's education of the mouth. No matter the challenge, developing the communication through the bit makes corrections available to me. The corrections will help me support the horse as he is learning to put a workable canter together.

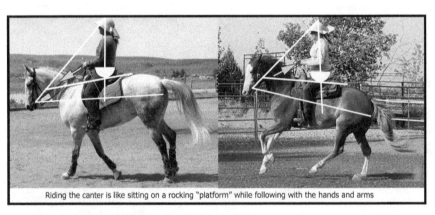

Riding the canter is like sitting on a rocking "platform" while following with the hands and arms

In my experience, the canter is more than staying on and galloping through fields of flowers. It's a nice image but the reality is that we want to "play our instrument" equally well at all gaits. I included the illustrated photos to show the multitude of angle changes that happen throughout the canter stride between us and our horse. The vertical line through the rider's torso is the vertical equilibrium to be maintained. The lines from my head to the horse's mouth show how much the distance changes each stride. The horse's head and the contact ARE farther away, they don't just feel farther away. The line along the horse's back is the level of the "'sitting platform" that rocks while the horse canters. The half-moon represents my pelvis as it stays somewhat in the same place allowing the platform to change under it. The blue arrows show the movements of my hands as the distance from my torso to the horse's mouth changes. The line from the point of the horse's hip to the mouth can show overall balance (give or take).

I'm hoping that it will be a springboard for you to step up to the challenge of creating informative contact in this gait. The horses' gaits, both natural and more developed, add yet another layer of intricacy for riders to have to add to everything else they are already doing. The aids will need to be adjusted as the horse changes balance, flexion, gait, speed, posture.... This is the reason I wrote this work. Without the preparation, the understanding, the repetition of the aids between hand and mouth, we have little chance of riding artfully or even equitably. The education of the horse's mouth is the only fair and respectful path for the horse. And it is the only path that respects the art that has been riding and equitation for 500 plus years. Let's not let it fall to the wayside on our watch regardless of our goals with our horses.

Since this work does not cover riding position and technique specifically, I encourage you to seek resources to further your riding position. Here are a few to get started:

Centered Riding and *Centered Riding 2* by Sally Swift
The Dressage Seat by Anja Beran

11

Exercises for Contact

I don't want to leave you with information and motivation without some extra tools for refinement and practice. I've assembled a list of some of my favorite exercises you can do to improve your own coordination in the arms and hands. These exercises focus on bringing to attention an element that is important to our role in maintaining contact with your horse.

While we learn how to move with our horse and maintain a fluid connection, we also need to be aware of our tendency to be busy for the sake of busyness. This brings about meaningless movements in our hands that could be caused by nerves, habits, concentration, or the driving feeling that you "should be doing something." The goal is to do exactly what the horse needs, no more, no less.

The movement and limits of movements are like variations of scales that musicians play on their instruments. With enough repetition, the fingers and arms can articulate without thought. That is our goal. If your hands and arms are so well practiced at the movements required, you'll not only do them better, you will be able to focus instead on other things you want to do with your contact or position.

There are more activities you can do for fun and challenge like riding your horse while holding a plastic goblet filled with water or the classic "Egg and Spoon." You can even do these activities while walking, jogging, hiking, or going up and down stairs.

Exercises Without Your Horse

Trampoline Reins

I always enjoyed jumping on a trampoline. I was in gymnastics for some years and the trampoline felt a bit like flying. I still enjoy it today. One winter, I came up with this exercise when a teacher of mine said my hands weren't very stable. I thought to myself, "Well if I can move my body in different ways while keeping a set of 'reins' stable, that ought to make some improvement." My awareness of the changes I had to make within my joints to keep the reins snug quickly improved my ability to stay connected in the contact.

On a trampoline or a jog tramp, fix a light rope (or reins if you have extra) to the frame of the trampoline or nearby fixed object. When you begin to bounce, even slightly, the fixed reins will tell your arms and hands what to do to stay connected. If you don't follow, you're not going to be bouncing!

After you get used to the basic coordination of the exercise, try challenging yourself to jump a bit higher, twist your hips, or

Keeping the "reins" from swinging while I bounce

jump from side to side. The ultimate goal is to keep the reins from swinging at all while you are bouncing.

It is excellent exercise and it can inform and strengthen the muscles in your arms. You will begin to be able to do something entirely different with your arms and hands than you are doing with your body and not have to concentrate so hard to accomplish it.

The Hand Spring

Opening and closing the hand one finger at a time

To practice the articulation of the fingers, tie a pair of reins to a fixed object like a post or a ring on the wall with a bungee cord. Hold the reins as you prefer (with three or four fingers around the rein). Open and close your fingers one at a time in order (pinky, ring, middle, and vice versa). The pointer finger and the thumb stay closed to be the anchor point to the lenght of the reins. Start slowly concentrating on a true one at a time movement. Speed up when it feels easy and fluid.

Another exercise is to repeatedly open and close each finger in order as you go. Open and close the ring finger a few times, leave it relaxed while you open and close the middle finger a few times.

You can do this work with one hand at a time or both hands at once. Repeat more often with your less dominant hand until it feels equally dexterous with your dominant hand.

Exercises On Your Horse

With any of the exercises under saddle please be sure your horse is quiet and controllable. You want to be safe to be able to focus on your exercises. If you are in doubt, one solution would be to ride a "school horse" to practice or to have a "lunge lesson" where someone has you on a lunge line while you ride and practice.

Cavesson Riding

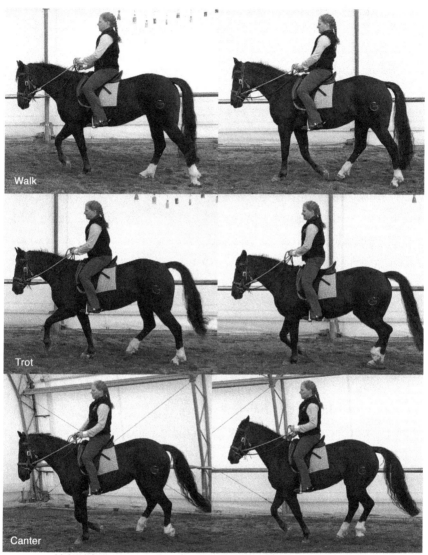

Maintaining contact on the cavesson rein in the walk, trot and canter

Riding with a set of reins to the cavesson is a great way to allow the horse to teach you how to follow the movements of his head. You can make mistakes, get a bit out of rhythm and have a more obvious contact with the cavesson without frustrating the horse.

If your horse is safe to ride with a soft cavesson, you could ride these exercises with that alone. If not, riding with a cavesson under a bridle is the safer bet. You could also put reins to the lunging cavesson and ride a lunge lesson practicing keeping steady contact that way.

I hold the cavesson rein and regular rein between different fingers

By riding with your bridle rein looser than your cavesson rein (or riding with only your cavesson rein), you can get a lot of practice following the movements of the head and neck that very closely simulates the movement you will be following in the mouth. It will have less complexity because we have removed the spring systems of the mouth and jaw but it is the closest we can get.

Riding with a Neck Rope

A neck rope is simply a slender rope put around a horse's neck. I like to tie knots in mine to keep the rope from sliding through my fingers. The neck rope is another way to lead the movement of the hands in direct correlation to the movement of the horse's neck. Where the neck goes, the hands go.

I put the rope and my reins through different fingers so I can clearly feel when I am out of sync with my horse. The finger holding the neck rope will feel the changing pressure on the neck rope signaling me that my neck rope is not remaining steady. Therefore my hands are not remaining steady in relation to the horse.

How I carry a neck rope with my reins

Riding with the neck rope at the trot (above) and canter (below)

The idea is with a lifting action more or less toward your nose, keep the neck rope snug against the base of the horse's neck. With our body, we are coordinating our movements to the horse's torso while our hands are moving with the horse's neck. This is part of the educational benefit of all these exercises. Teaching and repeating so that our mind and body can begin to do disparate things at the same time. The old "pat your head and rub your tummy" idea.

In the photo (left) I am lifting the neck rope while still able to follow the movement of the contact and give back to my horse in a forward direction. This is a unique benefit of riding with a neck rope compared to the other exercises.

With a neck rope I can maintain contact with the horse

Trotting with a neck rope is a useful way for the rider to be aware that the hands do not rise and fall as the rider posts. The hands match the horse, which does not change a lot on the vertical plane in relationship with the rider in the trot. There are not many other ways to experience this dissociation of movements without riding and using exercises like this one.

The benefit of riding with the neck rope at the canter is learning how much "following" it takes to maintain a contact that coordinates well with the horse's body. Many riders follow either too much or too little interrupting the balance of the horse.

Stick Riding

I can hear the collective groans of my students when I say the words "Stick Riding." There are two versions of this exercise for two different purposes.

The best "sticks" are either PVC pipe, wooden dowel, or metal pipe between 20"-24" in length. The length depends on the width you carry your hands apart. Since I believe riding with your hands the width apart of your ribs, that brings us to about two feet.

Both positions, if the horse is reliable enough, can be ridden in the walk, trot, and canter. At first, do what you can and keep growing as you become more comfortable.

The first position (top right) is to hold the stick with your thumbs as you hold your reins normally. Riding with the stick like this helps with people who tend to ride with

The two positions for stick riding

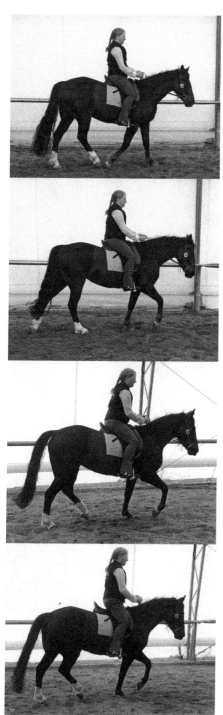
Balancing the stick on my wrists in the walk and trot

their hands too close together or tip their thumbs too much toward one another.

The second position, (previous page lower photo) is balancing the stick on your wrists. This position is more advanced and demanding of the balance of the rider. The contact is not maintained so you can either ride your horse on a looser rein or have someone lunge your horse while you ride.

Balancing the stick on your wrists as your body moves with the horse is a way of vastly improving your proprioception (perception or awareness of the position and movement of the body). It is difficult and many dropped sticks occur during practice. I won't make you get off your horse to retrieve your stick every time you drop it but it is a great incentive for my students!

The canter is a big challenge as there is so much motion happening. The horse is going faster and we have to make adjustments more quickly to stay in balance. This photo series (right) illustrates the positive effect of the balancing stick on the stability of the arm position in the canter.

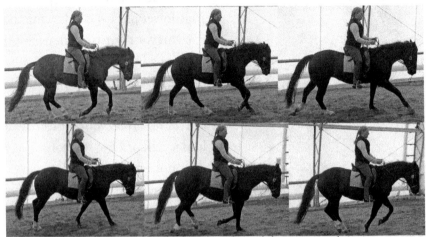

Cantering while balancing the stick on my wrists

If we can balance and coordinate our movements to the level where we can balance a loose stick on our wrists, we are approaching the level of what could be called the "independent seat." The independent seat is one that can match well the movements of the horse beneath in all gaits and movements. It is stable and quiet, merging the horse and rider into a unison of balance and movement.

Perhaps we should refer to the "independent hand" instead. A hand that can match all the movements of the horse's mouth in all directions. A hand that matches the exact amount of pressure regardless of what the horse offers.

Perhaps it is a chicken and egg conundrum where the beginning is not as clear as might be believed. Perhaps it is cross-pollination where each improves the other. I find this most likely.

In this book, I wanted to give you the information to move forward on your journey to the "gallant mouth" for whatever activities you are want to pursue. The gallant mouth takes time, knowledge, and application of that knowledge in a way that respects the horse.

We must never forget that the gallant mouth is the mirror image of the gallant hand. Let's continue the pursuit of these inseparable marvels. Let's honor the centuries of ecuyers who furthered the technical and artistic discoveries having worked tirelessly to pass them on to us.

12

The Code

Keep to The Code

Sounds like it should be said in a pirates' voice but I think of a Code as a system in which everything is in accord. Everything is in harmony. And in the age of computer coding, it is well known that if the Code isn't inputted correctly, the program doesn't work.

Most of the Code I keep to could be ascribed to the influence of the French tradition. Some of it is what I have learned along the way. So what does a Code really mean when it comes to the horses, the riders, and their education?

- For a Code to work, all the pieces must be in agreement. From the groundwork of a yearling all the way to the highest level of training I am working on the same overarching goals using similar aids and mindset throughout.
- The Code is consistently and persistently reinforced. If not, it's more of a suggestion. The horse will only learn the Code if he experiences the same request followed by the same consequences. Those consequences can be positive or negative: a rewarding Reprieve or continued Request. Consequences need not be punitive.

- The Code itself and learning the Code should make sense to both horse and rider. Along with consistency, the Code needs to be broken down into achievable pieces appropriate for the pair, their ages, and their stage of learning.
- The Code is beneficial for all horses and all activities. If not, it is simply training. Training to run fast or stop hard. Training to track a cow or lope low and slow. A Code supersedes all disciplines and improves the overall function and usability of every horse.
- The Code is beneficial for each individual horse. The horse has a right to ask, "What's in it for me?" He didn't ask to be ridden. He didn't ask to be bred, bought, or sold. I've heard people say, "I feed him so he can do what I want for 1 hour out of 24." Maybe. It might depend on what you ask him to do. If what you're asking him to do creates balance, relaxation, symmetry, and strength, the horse is likely to actively participate in the activity. If the hour per day involves activities that are counter to the horse's nature, demeaning, or harm the horse physically or mentally, that's another story. Probably another book.
- The Code is logical in its sequences working from simple to complex in its entirety.
- The Code takes the physical, mental, and emotional well-being of the horse in mind. The Code reevaluates regularly along the path of education and adjusts accordingly.
- The Code offers a variety of learning paths for the variety of equine and human learners.
- The Code looks upon the horse and rider as a complete beings, both in and out of the arena. Adequate nutrition, suitable physical and emotional wellness, and basic medical care are all part of those who follow a Code. None of it needs to be fancy, but all the participants need to be adequately healthy.

- The Code utilizes tools that are respectful. Tack designed to cause pain in order to gain obedience is not part of any positive Code.
- The Code doesn't include bullying. Intelligent interaction with horses and riders puts aside force and seeks interaction and understanding.
- The Code offers grace to both horse and rider. Perfection is unattainable but forgiveness and encouragement are forever at hand. There is always another ride, another try, another day. Take a breath. Smile. Have another go.
- The Code grows and adjusts with personal advancement and further physical and mental health. Some aspects of the Code will shift in meaning and importance along the way. This is as it should be.
- The Code grows and adjusts with scientific advancement and further education. A useful Code cannot be written in stone.

The Code

Above all, preserve the nobility of the horse • Request, Reprieve, Resist, Release • Separate the aids for clarity before combining them • Hands control the mouth, neck, and shoulders. Legs control the haunches and impulsion • Inviting Rein, Neck Rein, Neutral Rein • Lift the hands instead of pull • A horse behind the bit will soon be behind the leg • Stretch the neck laterally for relaxation and straightness • Shift the Shoulders for the mobility of the forehand • The neck position affects the overall balance of the horse • Follow the mouth until the horse can follow the hand • Demi arret for lifting the neck, opening the poll, or lightening the contact • Descente de main to reward and check the balance • Beware the toll of poll flexion • La detente-relaxation in the warm up • The horse becomes steady then the hand becomes steady, not the other way round • Légèreté-to have a progressively lighter Request for the same or greater Response • Both legs Request freely and energetically forward • Work with the nature of the horse, not against it • Anything forced can never be beautiful • Position before action • Lateral movements are to be used for a purpose • A steady hand keeps steady contact • Legs back for reinback and collection • If there is nothing to do, do nothing • If it is too hard for the horse, it isn't useful • Prepare your horse for every request • Perfect transitions are the key to collection • For any student to learn the lesson, he must know the words • Collection is a great desire to go with very little going • Légèreté places the responsibility on the rider to make things easy for the horse • Descente des aides puts the horse on parole • The curb bit is the longitudinal flexor and extender, the snaffle the lateral flexor and elevator • Descente de Jambes to test the horse's impulsion and energy • The education of the horse begins when you first look at him • We take responsibility for what the horse needs to feel comfortable in the mouth with a bit • Hyperflexion has no place in intelligent equitation • Active and Passive Touch • Correcting asymmetry for healthier movement is a responsibility of the rider • A horse cannot be above the contact if the hand remains above the mouth • The contact affects every part of the horse's body • Start from the simple, proceed to the complex • Teach from the ground, continue from the back • One request, one response. Repeat. • Better is better • The best gymnastic is mental, then physical • Correct the cause, not the effect • Calm, forward, and straight • Artful riding in combination with nature makes the horse more beautiful •

<<Demander: Le bonheur consiste à se contenter de peu>>
"Request: Happiness comes from being satisfied with little.

Baucher

L'Légèreté

POSTSCRIPT

If you bought this book, thank you for your curiosity! If you actually read this whole book, I'm impressed! I tend to be both long-winded and long-headed, wanting to know and apply everything I can learn. I can overwhelm people with my enthusiasm for information but it's information I hope will help you in your equestrian journey.

Something I didn't talk about in The Code which I will briefly discuss here is leg aids. I wanted to focus on the hand and its importance but as you interact with the information in this work, you will want to ride. Part of The Code is "separation of the aids." That means a couple of things. 1. The hands control the mouth, neck, and shoulders. The legs control the hindquarters. 2. Both legs applied where they naturally hang, indicate to the horse to freely and fairly energetically go forward. 3. A single leg applied in the same place indicates to the horse to move the haunches in the opposite direction.

In the next work I write, if such a work is desired, I will talk about the actions of the legs and how they work with the actions of the hands to create longitudinal and lateral changes of balance. When we have a fine-tuned Code with the horse in this way, we approach preparing them for collection. We have also created a Code that is functional for all kinds of riding activities: recreational, working, or exhibiting.

Academy of Defense. "A Chronology of American Cavalry Saber Manuals" https://academyofdefence.com/cavalry-manuals/

Baucher, François, "New Method of Horsemanship and Dialogues on Equitation." JA Allen & Company Limited. 1992

Beaudant, Etienne. "Horse Training Outdoors and High School." Charles Scribner's Sons 1931, Xenophon Press LLC 2014

Beran, Anja. "The Dressage Seat." Trafalgar Square Books. English translation 2017.

Cavendish, William "A General System of Horsemanship", Trafalgar Square books, 2012, ©JA Allen, 2000 reproduced from 1743 edition.

Corniani, Guilia, and Hannes P Saal. "Tactile Innervation Densities across the Whole Body." Journal of Neurophysiology, no. 124, ser. 4, 19 Oct. 2020, pp. 1229–1240. 4.

De Bussigny, Henry L. "Equitation." The Riverside Press, 1922

Decarpentry, General Albert. "Piaffer and Passage" English Translation 1975, Arco Publishing Company Inc.

Eldrønd, Vibeke Sødring, Dr. Krasnodebska, Marta Julia. Harrison, Adrian. IKVH, Faculty of Health & Medical Sciences "MULTI-FREQUENCY BIOIMPEDANCE AND MYOFASCIAL RELEASE THERAPY: AN EQUINE "ATLASORANGE1" VALIDATION STUDY" Gronnegaardsvej 7, 1870 Frederiksberg C, Denmark. © 2015, Knowledge Enterprises, Inc.

"Equitation in the French Tradition" Inscribed in 2011 on the Representative List of the Intangible Cultural Heritage of Humanity. https://ich.unesco.org/en/RL/equitation-in-the-french-tradition-00440

Fillis, James. "Breaking and Riding." J.A. Allen and Co Ltd. 1969, reprint of original 1902

"French Equitation Inscribed on the UNESCO Intangible Heritage Representative List" www.eurodressage.com 11/28/2011

Froissard, Jean. "A Guide to Basic Dressage." Lyons Press edition, 2005.

Froissard, Jean. "Classical Horsemanship for Our Time." Jean Froissard and Lily Powell, First Lyons Press edition, 2005.

Froissard, Jean. "Equitation." A.S. Barnes and Co., Inc. 1967.

Goff, Dr Lesley, PhD, Musculoskeletal and Animal Physiotherapist. "The Hype About the Hyoid" Aug 16, 2020, Printed in July-Augus 2020 issue of Horses and People Magazine

Hancock, Elise, "A Handy Guide to Touch." Johns Hopkins Magazine Electronic Edition April 1995, https://pages.jh.edu/jhumag/495web/touch.html

Jousseaume, André. "Progressive Dressage" English Translation 1978, JA Allen and company Limited .

Karl, Philippe. "Twisted Truths of Modern Dressage." Cadmos Verlag GmbH, Brunsbek 2008/2009

Kirjorinne, Niina. "The Dilemma of Pads and Nosebands." www.eurodressage.com, Thu 2/03/2022. Photos by Stefan Westerback, Niina Kirjorinne, Silke Rottermand, Astrid Appels. https://eurodressage.com/2022/02/03/dilemma-pads-and-nosebands

de Kerbrech, Faverot. "Methodical Dressage of the Riding Horse." Xenophon Press 2010
KTH The Royal Institute of Technology. (2013, September 16). Feeling small: Fingers can detect nano-scale wrinkles even on a seemingly smooth surface. ScienceDaily. Retrieved January 21, 2022 from www.sciencedaily.com/releases/2013/09/130916110853.htm

L'Hotte, General Alexis-François. "Questions Équestres." Trans. Hilda Nelson.1997. Original French publishing date 1895.

La Bibliothèque Mondiale du Cheval, "La photo du galop arrière" (The Photo of the Canter Backward) https://labibliothequemondialeducheval.org/en/archives/2429

de la Guérinière, François Robichon. "Ecole de cavaleri tome premier" 1736, Paris de La Guéreinière, François Robichon. "A Treatise Upon Horsemanship," Captain William Frazer translation. Hircarrah Press, 1801.

de a Guérinière, François Robichon. "The School of Horsemanship Part II" Xenophon Press, 1992.

de Lagarenne, George "Dressage of the Outdoor Horse, Recalled by one of his (Kerbrech) students." Xenophon Press, 2010

Lesté-Lasserre, Christa, MA. "Equine TMJ Changes Common, but Clinical Signs Rare." Feb 21, 2020. The Horse Magazine-Copyright 2022 The Horse Media Group LLC.

Les Amis du Cadre Noir (no author listed) "Capitaine Saint Phalle" https://amisducadrenoir.fr/le-cadre-noir-de-saumur/les-grands-ecuyers-du-cadre-noir/capitaine-saint-phalle/

Linton, Alexa. Osteopath, Kinesiologist, Equine Sports Therapist. "Demystifying the Cranial Bones," www.Horse journals.com April 11, 2018. Originally published Nov/Dec 2017 Canadian Horse Journal.

Mellor DJ. Mouth Pain in Horses: Physiological Foundations, Behavioural Indices, Welfare Implications, and a Suggested Solution. Animals. 2020; 10(4):572. https://doi.org/10.3390/ani10040572

Nelson, Hilda. "Alexis-François L'Hotte: The Quest for Lightness in Equitation." JA Allen & Company Limited. 1997.

Nelson, Hilda. "François Baucher: The Man and His Method". Xenophon Press LLC 2013

Nevzorov, Alexander. "Dressage: Let's Dot the I's and Cross the T's." Haute Ecole Equine Anthology, 2009, pp. 30–43.

Nguyen JD, Duong H. Anatomy, Shoulder and Upper Limb, Hand Arteries. [Updated 2021 Sep 3]. In: StatPearls [Internet]. Treasure Island(FL):StatPearls Publishing; 2022 Jan-. Available from: https://www.ncbi.nlm.nih.gov/books/NBK546583/

Paillard, Jean Saint-Fort. "Understanding Equitation." Doubleday and Co, Inc. Published in Great Britain by Pitman Publishing Ltd. 1975

Papyrus Museum of Venice "Oldest Manuscript of Xenophon's Hellenica" https://www.onb.ac.at/en/museums/papyrus-museum

Pluvinel, Antoine. "Le Manege Royal." 1989 English translation J.A. Allen & Co Ltd. London. 2015 English translation Xenophon Press LLC. Based on 1626 edition.

Racinet, Jean-Claude. "Racinet Explains Baucher." Xenophon Press 1997

Rottermann, Silke. "History of French Equitation - Part I: Dressage a la Francaise" Eurodressage, www.eurodressage.com 9/13/2014

Rotterman, Silke. "History of French Equitation - Part II: Modern French Classical Equitation.". www.eurodressage.com 10/16/2014

Rottermann, Silke. "History of French Equitation - Part III: Tradition Does Not Exclude Love for Progress." www.eurodressage.com 11/10/2014.

Rottermann, Silke. "Cadre Noir, French Treasure of Horsemanship." www.eurodressage.com 4/25/2011

Rotterman, Silke and Carde, Christian. "Walk: The Queen of Gaits: Colonel Christian Card shares this classical approach to training the horse." Dressage Today via www.dressagetoday.com Original: Sept 30, 2014. Updated Feb 5, 2019.

Rotterman, Silke. "Noesband Special: Part 1: The History of the Noseband." Eurodressage. Tue, 02/07/2012 - 09:36. https://www.eurodressage.com/2012/02/07/noseband-special-part-i-history-noseband

Swift, Sally. "Centered Riding." Trafalgar Square Farm Book. 1985

Swift, Sally. "Centered Riding 2, Further Exploration." Trafalgar Square Publishing. 2002

Tomassini, Giovanni Battista. "The Italian Tradition of Equestrian Art," 2014 Xenophon Press

United Nations Educational, Scientific and Cultural Organization. Intangible Cultural Heritage. https://ich.unesco.org/en/

PHOTO CREDITS:

The hands of the hand collage in Chapter 2:

- Adrienne Hendricks, saddle maker, Adrienne Hendricks Saddlery, Eagle, ID. https://englishsaddle.com

- CJ Wilkinson, Bladesmith-Emmett, ID. www.ceejw.com
- Paul Tillitson-Jazz Pianist (deceased). Wood River, ID. Please check out his music on iTunes, YouTube and Spotify.
- Tim Waddle-Head chef and creator of everything on the menu at Italianesque, Nampa, ID. Owned by Tim and his wife Paula. https://italianesque.business.site
- Louise Owen-Violinist and chocolatier in NY, NY.
- Joanna Robertson-Licensed Massage Therapist, Kindred Therapeutic Massage, Meridian, ID.
- David Eames-Farrier, New Plymouth, ID.
- Dr. James Thomson (retired), Emmett, ID.

The lion's share of technical photographs were patiently taken by interns Katie Sutliff and Elli VanDerLinde. Meanwhile, intern Kayla Von Bergen kept the farm running.

Professional photographs artistically and graciously provided by:

- Ashton Kingsley Photography "Capturing the Heart and Soul of the Horse." San Luis Obisbo County, CA. www.ajskphotography.com
- Kelvin Watkins Photography Salem, OR. www.kelvinwatkinsphotography.com

My saddle was custom-made by Master Saddler Suzie Fletcher of Oxfordshire, England. I'm greatly honored to have such a masterpiece to ride in every day. www.suziefletcher.co.uk

Linda Kaye Hollingsworth-Jones has lived at Willow Grove since 1992 with her husband Steve and (now grown) sons Cation and Adarsh. The menagerie includes horses, dogs, cats, chickens, ducks, and geese. She continues to train horses of all kinds and maintains an internship program for future equine professionals at Willow Grove.

Willow Grove is the home of the Willow Grove Conservatory for Equestrian Studies as well as the critically endangered Hackney Horse.

You can find out more about Willow Grove at www.willowgroveidaho.com

CPSIA information can be obtained
at www.ICGtesting.com
Printed in the USA
BVHW010555110422
633918BV00004BA/110